2 Losey on Losey

Losey on Losey

Edited and introduced by Tom Milne

London

Secker & Warburg in association with the
British Film Institute

The Cinema One Series is published by
Martin Secker & Warburg Limited
14 Carlisle Street London W1
in association with *Sight and Sound*
and the Education Department of the
British Film Institute, 81 Dean Street London W1

General Editors
Penelope Houston and Tom Milne (*Sight and Sound*)
Peter Wollen (Education Department)

Losey on Losey by Joseph Losey
first published by Martin Secker & Warburg 1967
is a *Sight and Sound* publication

SBN 436 09854 7 (hardcover)
436 09855 5 (paperback)

Reprinted with revisions 1968

Designed by Farrell/Wade

Printed in Great Britain by
Jarrold and Sons Limited, Norwich

Contents

Front cover: Jacqueline Sassard in *Accident*

Introduction

To each his own Losey. There are those who sigh nostalgically for the directness and simplicity of his beginnings in *The Boy With Green Hair* and *The Dividing Line*; those who feel that for purity and boldness of *mise en scène*, films like *Time Without Pity* or *The Criminal* will never be equalled; and those for whom the story of Losey starts with the revelation of a master in *The Servant*.

My own view—and the only reason for going into it here is to explain the attitude which dictated the questions put to Losey in this book—is that there has been a steady, recognisable progress from *The Boy With Green Hair* to *Accident*. As the French critic Gilles Jacob put it: "If it is true that, fundamentally, a Losey film traces the passage of a character from darkness to light, the same image might be applied to his own career, built over twenty years upon a series of experiments constantly redirected towards a more precise understanding of his art. In this respect the prime Losey hero is Losey himself, who seems destined to be remembered less for his mutilated body of work—a sort of dress rehearsal for an ideal film which never materialises—than for his intellectual journeying in search of a style." (This was written early in 1966, and to my mind that ideal film has now materialised in *Accident* —but that's another story.)

I said a 'recognisable progress', but this of course is hindsight. At the time, what one might call the later middle-period films (*The Criminal*, *The Damned*, *Eve*) were something of a puzzlement:

Filming *Modesty Blaise*: Losey and Monica Vitti

Losey and *King and Country*

hypnotic, brilliant, but somehow over-eager, over-crowded, and for that very reason occasionally inclined to slip into bathos. Neither they, nor the very much more uneven first British films, seemed to bear any relationship to the Hollywood Losey, who lingered on in the mind as a maker of films which were direct, unhurried, and, above all, dominated by space: wide, empty streets and barren landscapes in *The Dividing Line*; the bare white walls of the Spanish house in *The Prowler*; the landscape of stone and concrete in *M*. Seeing these films again, one realises that this impression of limitless, airy space is not strictly accurate; that the child murderer in *M*, for instance, is not really alone in the concrete jungle of the garage during his final trial by underworld, but only seems to be because he is so cunningly *selected* from his background. This of course, as Losey explains in the course of the interview which follows, is the whole point of his 'pre-design' work with John Hubley and Richard MacDonald.

But in the early British films, with their bravura angles and effects, Losey seemed to have opted for mannerism in place of selectivity. Retrospectively, however, it becomes clear that Losey was going through a process of evolution, adapting his style to a new, more probing, much warier realisation of the complexity of people and problems; and the 'mannerism' was a symptom of his attempt to encompass this new vision. The process was not helped by the fact that, right up to *Eve*, Losey was forced to work on subjects not of his choice which therefore had to be pushed, coaxed or forced into shape. But by the time of *The Servant* the style has matured, and Losey's bravura camera was completely at the service of his vision.

To put it rather crudely (there are all sorts of reservations, but it makes my point), the difference between the British films before and after *The Servant* is that *before*, selectivity means pointing out what you are supposed to see; *after*, it means withdrawing what you are not supposed to see. In *Time Without Pity*, for instance, one is forced to become aware of the split-level apartment with Goya bull on the wall which characterises the bullying Stanford; in *Accident*, the cosy domestic muddle of Stephen's house—a reflection, if one cares to make the connection, of his state of indecision—is simply *there*.

With *Accident*, in fact, Losey comes full circle back to the simplicity of *The Boy With Green Hair*. But there is simplicity and simplicity; and for *Accident*, perhaps lucidity is a better word to describe the serene ease with which Losey controls and organises its very complex themes and characters. Looking 'lucid' up in *Chambers's Dictionary*, I find, as it happens, an enchanting definition of *Accident* itself: "Shining: transparent: easily understood: intellectually bright: not darkened with madness."

The text of this book is taken from a series of taped interviews with Losey, done in a fairly concentrated period of about ten days. The opinions expressed are sometimes definitive, more often spontaneous and therefore necessarily of the moment. Many things by the very nature of the form have been omitted. In particular

Accident: Losey and Vivien Merchant

some colleagues not mentioned might be hurt by omission of their names. This is in no way intentional on Losey's part, but merely the result of the discursive and somewhat random format.

As the interviews took place very shortly after *Accident* had opened in London, the film naturally loomed large in both Losey's mind and mine. Our starting-point was a suggestion of mine that a case could be made for there being a second accident at the end of the film. After seeing Anna (Jacqueline Sassard) off to the airport, Stephen (Dirk Bogarde) walks through the empty Oxford cloisters alone, and the cut to the last scene with the children in front of his house is bridged by the sound of a car about to crash. Obviously this sound is intended as an echo in Stephen's mind; on the other hand, the dog which has been playing with the children before they enter the house and the door is closed, runs down to the road just before the car actually crashes. The idea of the dog as a symbol—or at least as a notorious cause of accidents —had not occurred to Losey; and it was this which sparked off the reflections on the shooting. of this sequence which open the interview.

1: Interpretations

Your films have always roused very strange and very varied critical interpretations, particularly in France: Pierre Rissient's recent book, for example, argues in effect that you have never really matched the high achievement of your first two films. Some of these interpretations may merely be misguided; others arise because, in trying to dig deeper into the films, a critic may misinterpret your intentions or find something you never intended—a recent example might be the role of the dog in the last sequence of Accident. *Do you find all these interpretations and misinterpretations disturbing?*

When I first came to Europe, nobody knew much about my Hollywood films, and there was no particular reason why they should: I had made five films there in five years, with two years between *The Boy With Green Hair* and the rest, so the last four were made in something less than three years. Also, a second depression came just at the moment when the most successful of my Hollywood films, *The Prowler*, was appearing, and there was a great reduction in cinema consumption and film audiences; so while that film and the others were successful, they weren't successful in the enormous way of the early Forties, even the late Thirties or early Fifties. So Rissient and other students in France came to be familiar with some of my films long before people did in either the United States or England. Why this is I don't know, except that there seems to me to be—and always has been—a far more

The Damned: Shirley Ann Field, Macdonald Carey

active and on the whole more informed interest in films in France than elsewhere.

The curious thing about these discoverers of my early films was they were not interested in the content; most of them were in total disagreement not only with me but with each other as to what the films said and what they led to. I don't really know what interested them, as I found myself lumped with Howard Hawks or Samuel Fuller, or any one of a number of directors whose work I may like, respect or not, but who seem to have little to do with me or my work. This passionate advocacy of my films was extremely valuable and helped me to begin again, to regain confidence; but it soon became a handicap, because very often the films were valued, and I was valued, for what seemed to me the wrong reasons. Also, as so often happens with the young and the fanatical, there was the stigma—and it is a stigma—of the clique, of the cult. This put a

Prison bars in *The Servant*

great many serious people off, and I think this was right. There also arose a kind of possessiveness which is the penalty of involvement with the extremely young and immature: I couldn't do anything they didn't approve of without somehow being a betrayer. I felt I owed them a good deal, as indeed I did, and I tried as much as I could to respect this obligation and help them. That was a mistake, and I'm through with it.

Interpretation and intention is a different matter. In a curious way I think that films, perhaps much more so than novels, very often have levels of which the director may not be entirely conscious. While it seems to me that a novelist *must* be conscious of his levels, I'm not sure a director always is—in fact I'm sure I often am not. For instance, I received a letter from a Frenchman working in Algeria with the Cinémathèque just after he had seen *Accident* at the London press show; a long letter about what *Accident* had meant to him, even though he hadn't understood all of the dialogue. Most of it had never occurred to me, and most of it was certainly not consciously intended, but almost all of it was something I believe, that is part of me, and which perhaps therefore *was* conveyed: it certainly conveyed itself to him—mostly in this particular instance it was a question of relationships of men to women and women to men, and men to men as against men and women, which is something I am deeply concerned with.

I have also frequently come across the unearthing of similarities in my pictures, particularly among the younger devotees. One critic, for instance, noted that the bars of the staircase in *The Servant* were a prison and recalled *The Criminal*—though obviously this wasn't any part of my intention. Very frequently they find symbols, even sexual symbols, which are certainly not intended. When I first began to make films, and even later, I did consciously work with symbols, but for quite some years I have equally consciously tried to stay away from any I see; and it's surprising how often something absolutely unintended, arising sometimes from the problems of film-making, turns out to be picked up.

For instance in *Eve*, which was a very carefully planned picture, there was a good deal I had intended to shoot which for various reasons I couldn't. At one point there is a sequence in which the Welsh writer has gone to bed with a girl, and the transition to morning is a gushing fountain in the middle of one of the Roman squares. Originally this was a very carefully planned transition, which was supposed to be a high shot starting on something quite different and coming down to the fountain. I was never able to shoot it, so found I had no transition there. Rather than put in a dissolve—which I loathe: it slows, muddles and muddies—I used this shot which I had also used somewhere else (something I seldom do). It never occurred to me that anyone would take it as a sexual comment, like fireworks after an orgasm or whatever. But this was precisely the way it was taken, and many people fastened on it as a criticism of the intentional symbolism of the film. There was certainly an overall symbolism in relation to Venice and mirrors and water, but the fountain shot was *not* so intended. It was simply

Eve: Mirrors and Jeanne Moreau

an expedient, necessary because of the conditions of shooting.

So far as *Accident* is concerned, part of the first plan I worked out with Harold Pinter was that the accident would not be seen; it would be heard, and one would see the result afterwards; there would be a highly formal style of cutting established in the very first sequence, indicating to the audience that the film wasn't going to follow an exact continuity of time; and we would then somehow complete the circle of the film. Although Stephen finally returns to the life he has left and nearly destroyed, he returns as a changed man. He has hitherto always unburdened his guilts by half-telling them to his wife or to his friend Charley, and never could really contain even his unperformed acts within himself; but in this particular instance—the one night with the girl, Anna—although he has telegraphed it before, when it actually happens he will never

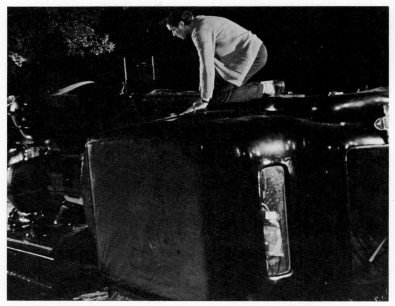

Accident: Dirk Bogarde

speak of it to Charley, he will never imply it to his wife, but he will live with it for all of his life. In other words he is a changed man, and therefore our intention was to come back to precisely the same soundtrack at the end—the car approaching and crashing—as a memory if you like, as part of his life from now on.

I think, by the way, the soundtrack of *Accident* is an exceptionally good one. I want to say this emphatically because it was the first job of sound editing by a young man named Alan Bell, and he did an extremely good job. However, I feel the sound of the car is a failure. I don't think it's his fault, but simply that Harold Pinter and I planned to sustain the crescendo of the car over a longer period of time than a film soundtrack can accommodate. Ideally, if I'd had all the money in the world, I would have shot the opening sequence with a helicopter on a car travelling too fast through country roads, the helicopter a little ahead of it and not much above it, and then have lost the car and come down into a static position on the house just before the crash is heard. That way there would have been an increasing excitement and crescendo, which I don't think sound alone can do because both the decibel range and the reproduction range are too limited. Anyway, we had to cheat a bit on the car. We used a high-powered sports car rather than a vintage high-powered one—technicians will recognise the difference, but the real thing simply didn't work at all.

The soundtrack is precisely the same at the end as at the beginning, and it was started over the cloister. In fact I took the music and the bells out over the cloister completely, so there would be no doubt in anybody's mind that this was not intended as a realistic effect. How could there be the sound of an approaching car about to crash over an evening cloister in Oxford, which then crashes in the afternoon by a country house? I also thought the two tracks would be recognised as identical. Obviously I overestimated what people remember of soundtracks, and what the ear absorbs when they are also seeing something visual and are not particularly concentrating on it.

There are also various other things I might have done differently if I'd had time and money to experiment. For instance, one critic said he thought it was a bit banal to have the crash over the house: he had sensed it coming and hoped it would occur over the cloisters. This is right as an idea, but would probably have been even more incomprehensible to most people. Others who knew something about the intention of the film and saw it in rough cut said, "Don't put the sound of the car at the end because it is there anyway, you feel it." This perhaps also was right, but there was no chance to find out. I should also like to say that one of the failures of the picture is the main titles. Originally, in the rough cut, when we finally got the soundtrack over that shot of the house without the titles, it was far more effective. The titles were too heavy and tended to detract from the sense of mystery and doom.

The last point is something I suppose one ought not to reveal, but I think it's important for a serious audience to understand what the problems of film-making are, how much can be controlled and how much cannot. That last shot of the two children and Stephen going into the house with the dog and closing the door had to be shot in the evening; we had already run into trouble on schedule because of weather; I also had trouble with the children, because of course they will only do something so many times; and I had arranged it various ways so I was fairly sure the little girl would trip up, but it was our last day of shooting and I knew I was losing the light and couldn't do it more than once. The intention always was that the dog should go into the house with Stephen and the children, the door would close, and the final image would be the same as the first. If you look carefully at that shot—on which I only had one take—you will see that the dog comes up to the door, but for some reason is frightened. Dirk, professional as always, held the door just as long as he could, then thought we were going to lose the shot, and began to shut it just as the dog started to come in. So the dog then turned away again. I risked losing the entire shot, so I called the dog to the camera. Now it never occurred to me that anybody might think there was a second accident or that the dog was killed. But both points, I must say, have arisen occasionally since the film was shown.

If one compares Eve, The Servant *or* Accident *with some of your earlier films, what strikes one immediately is their density. If you make films like this in which every shot, every camera movement or angle counts, people are going to look for meanings, and perhaps go wrong. For instance, the opening track up to the house.*

This is all right so long as it doesn't become pretentious or precious. The opening and the close of the picture were very conscious, very particularly mine. I wanted a completely symmetrical house, a completely symmetrical frame, because I wanted a completely symmetrical and classical film; I wanted to have it go full circle, and I wanted to state that here, in this house, a number of human beings encountered some aspects of their separate and mutual lives, and that the accident was only . . . it was a tragedy

Accident: Michael York, Vivien Merchant, Dirk Bogarde, Stanley Baker

but not *the* tragedy. It was a catalyst, as the girl was a catalyst. And also (as perhaps in *King and Country*, where I wanted to make a film set in war in which no shots were fired except the shots of the execution), I wanted to make a film about an accident in which there was no physical violence, only the inner violence of what people feel and the violent results of their behaviour.

I think I always have a sense of the whole shape of a film when I begin, or at least I do if it is all going well and right; and that opening shot of *Accident* is clear enough. In *Eve*, I began with a circular movement, and the 'Adam and Eve' and the Biblical quotation, and ended with a reverse circular movement, and the 'Adam and Eve' and another Biblical quotation. In the case of *Accident*, we are outside the gates, outside the house a little, and when we begin to move in to what is going to happen there, or what is happening there, I slowly moved in until there was just the house and no gates; and at the end I started on the house, and moved slowly back until it included the gates and we were outside. Which is, if you like, simply visual and maybe too formal, but I enjoy that kind of formality. A style, to me, has to do with the completion of a piece of work. Somebody said something to me the other day which pleased me enormously. A colleague of mine, another director, had been to see *Accident*; he didn't like it, he found it cold, not about people, and he didn't know which of the characters he was supposed to feel sympathy for. So far as I'm concerned, you are supposed to feel sympathy with everybody in one way or another, and not with any particular person. Anyhow, this friend of mine commented, "It's cold or it's not cold depending on how you see it and how it affects you; but it's a whole piece, it's . . ."—to use his exact metaphor which delighted me—"it's like a stick, you can pick it up and shake it and it doesn't break." If this is true—when it's true—it is probably a matter of the whole pre-concept and execution, and the pre-concept must necessarily include visual and physical form.

Structurally the film is very clear: it's when one comes down to specific points that there may be different interpretations. For instance, the very romantic imagery during the accident—the moon, the startled horse, the shot of William and Anna behind the shattered window looking almost like babes in the wood.

I think basically I am a romantic, but most romantics who don't die young in this age either become cynics or at least qualified romantics. But basically I am a romantic—I'm a sucker, an emotional sucker. By that I mean I am easily a victim of emotion, and I have to be careful about it. To some extent I think I have achieved

Accident: Romantic imagery

a discipline—but of course it's romantic, the girl in the ostrich feathers, the white image, the moonlight. It was intended lyrically, it was intended poetically—and this is where I so enjoy and get so much from working with Harold Pinter, because he is a poet. Although we talked about it many times and worked it out together, when he sat down to write it he gave it a poetic and lyrical rhythm which was an enormous help to me. I wanted a few more images at the beginning, but they were eliminated because of budget; in fact I spent the better part of one night trying to shoot some cows, but they didn't behave!

To revert to my earlier point about the soundtrack going on longer, this is really a technical thing and I was asking too much of the sound. In order to cover titles, which are always at least a

Accident: Dirk Bogarde, Jacqueline Sassard →

minute and forty-five seconds, and in this case slightly longer, you have to do a bit more than the titles because it has to continue after; so we had to have more than two minutes, and you cannot within the physical range of sound film at this moment get a steady crescendo of identifiable sound with just one thing (essentially one thing, although we put many things into it) for that length of time. This is one of those things you are always learning. For instance, this is a digression but these are points you have to consider if you are working in what is essentially a mechanical medium, mechanical in reproduction at least: I know very well that as soon as a print gets a little bit old and brittle, or conversely if a film is 'green' and not sufficiently used, or if there is any inaccuracy in threading a print, you will get a quaver or a wow in the sound. Therefore it is extremely dangerous to use string instruments, to use even a solo piano or a solo violin, or a reed instrument. For *Accident* I wanted very much—and I am sure it was right for this picture—to use two harps. They are fairly safe because they're slightly untrue. But I wanted against this the agony and wail of the saxophone, which John Dankworth played himself—and by the way the score was mostly improvised, though carefully prepared. John and I talked about it, and the exact combination which finally emerged was his. I had originally suggested it should maybe be only one instrument or two: I was afraid we might be running a risk with the saxophone. He said no. Well, ninety per cent of the times I have seen *Accident* projected, the score has had a wow; in other words, it's gone flat, it's gone sharp, and it drives me out of my mind, though most people probably don't notice. I'm never going to make this mistake again; I'm never going to make this sound mistake again either. If I want to do this kind of sustained crescendo sound effect, then I will have to find some way of complementing it in terms of image without destroying the plan of what I'm doing. When I told you how I would have shot it if I'd had the money, this is an after-thought. But with the helicopter I could have started before titles and behind titles, and still have managed to land the helicopter in position to get the static shot of the house; I wouldn't have been able to move in, excepting possibly with a zoom.

You are obviously very conscious of the soundtrack and particularly the music in your films. Eve, for instance, you once said had camera movements conceived in terms of the music. Do you often conceive your films along these lines?

No, of course not. But *Eve* more than any other. As far as *Accident* is concerned there is nothing that was conceived musically. I knew I didn't want very much music, and that I wanted it not as background but as comment. I also knew I didn't want it to begin or end in any of the conventional ways. I have always paid a great deal of attention to score, although there are two or three pictures on which I wasn't able to control the score, and where I think it has done great damage to the film; and also one or two pictures where I did have control but where I think the scores are not successful.

The use of the Cleo Laine song in *The Servant*, for instance, was conceived before I shot the film. The idea was that there should be a song with lyrics which would be the only record ever played in the house because it was an obsessional thing; and the lyrics at various times would be differently phrased, have different meanings. There is a kind of progression through the film, musically and visually, from the expected to the totally unexpected, from the conventional to what was then at least pretty unconventional. Therefore the opening arrangement of saxophones and strings is a corny one intended to suggest, if not the Hollywood picture, at least a fairly familiar kind of opening, which gradually progresses into something quite different. The song itself was arranged in four different ways. The first time it was a Nelson Riddle type of arrangement *à la* Bing Crosby and sung in the same way; it progresses through this to trad, simple backing and trad jazz rendering of a blues, to almost total and intentional cacophony with a big arrangement at the end.

Although it was a small arrangement, music was very important in my version of *M*, where the child murderer played a toy flute and this was integrated in the score. There was also a very carefully planned score by Richard Bennett, I think one of the best I have

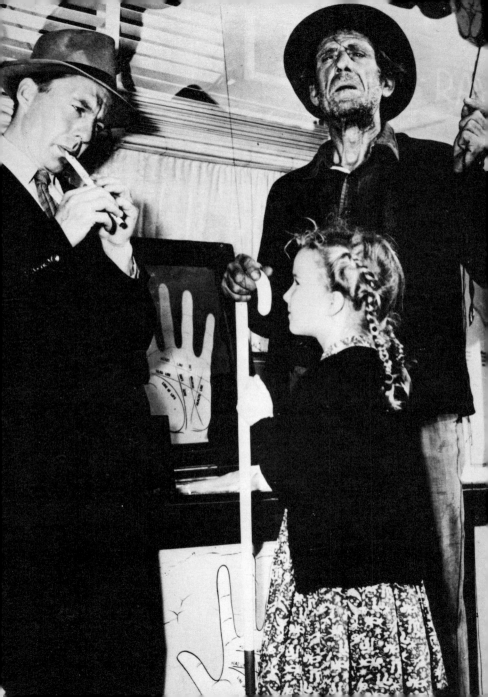

Eve: "Destruction and anguish"

ever had, for *Blind Date*; and another very carefully planned one, used in quite a different way, in the case of *The Criminal*, the first score for a feature John Dankworth had ever done. The third film I made, *The Prowler*, had a score by Lyn Murray which I worked on very hard and long; it still stands up, I think, and bears some relationship perhaps to the score of *The Criminal*, though it was scored for a more symphonic big band. On the other hand, there are certain films where the score isn't important. For instance, there is nothing except a double bass and a mouth organ in *King and Country*, and very little of that. As with *Accident*, it was largely improvised after the film was made.

With *Eve* I wanted to make a picture—as I still and always do—about the particular destruction and anguish and waste of most sexual relationships, whether heterosexual, homosexual, bisexual or whatever. Since the male character was essentially a phony, I

M: David Wayne, John Miljan and victim

Eve: Moreau and Billie Holiday

wanted to give him some kind of real background; and since the woman was fairly conventional, a prostitute at whatever price, I wanted to make her a woman who said virtually nothing but whom one sensed through the way she dressed, where she lived, what she had round her house, how she behaved privately, what she read, where she went when she was alone, etc. And there were a good many other sequences planned for the picture which are not there, including her visit to a confessional in the Catholic church—without words, nothing was ever said. When I went to speak to Jeanne Moreau about the film before I ever began it, I found her spending the summer in Brittany in a large hunting lodge. She was located in one small room with a very pleasant fire, surrounded by records in stacks on the floor, and they were all Billie Holiday.

As it happened Billie Holiday was someone I knew when she was sixteen; in fact, with John Hammond who later began her career and helped her at various points, I heard her singing in a speakeasy in Harlem when virtually nobody had heard of her. She had a terrifying kind of anguish, her autobiography is a terrifying document. (And this, by the way, is the book Jeanne Moreau is reading when she goes off by herself in the park. This is a detail, I don't care whether people notice it or not: it was important for me.) The score for *Eve* was to be a dialogue of different kinds of anguish and loneliness between a man and a woman. And Billie Holiday, in what she sang—because even when they were classic jazz songs, she changed the lyrics of most of the songs she sang—was the obvious choice, for me at any rate: both the heart-breaking quality of her voice and what she did with the words; and their familiarity too; and the kind of backing most of those records had. The other was Miles Davis, who is the most personal jazz musician I know. It was my intention to have him write a score with Gil Evans which would cross over the Billie Holiday records to become a kind of counterpoint and sometimes a duet—not words, just the instruments. He was interested, we talked about it, and the producers never made the arrangement. Because this was my intention, with my middle-aged romantic persistence—my persistence in romanticism into middle-age—I shot most of the film to Billie Holiday and Miles Davis records, with their rhythm, with that in my ear and with that intention. I finally wound up with twenty-three Billie Holiday cues, of which the producers finally cleared two, one of them not my first choice, and no Miles Davis.

Speaking about this at such length tends to derogate the score actually used in the film. This is not my intention, because it is one of the best scores I've ever had. It was written by Michel Legrand, a musician who in my opinion can be extraordinary—extraordinarily original and moving and special, and extraordinarily banal and bad. But he saw the film as I had finished it with the records, he knew what I wanted, he didn't resent it, and he set out in his own way to do it in his own terms, without embarrassment at what was already there, and at the same time achieving something original. People who have seen the film only in its emasculated

Eve: a sequence cut from most versions

version perhaps won't be able to judge Legrand's work for a variety of reasons.

In the first place it was a score planned from beginning to end with a progression, and certain sections have been cut out altogether; other sections have been transposed without any musical sense whatsoever. I never, if I can help it, except with very great purpose, use a dissolve or an optical; likewise in music I don't use fade-in and fade-out, which is the easiest non-creative solution to a creative problem. And the music has been faded in and out. The score was also closely related to very carefully planned sound effects which took me months and months to do, all of which were shot, and then recorded and mixed by the most brilliant technician in Rome. This was re-mixed, transposed, faded in and out, and it was cut. So, for me, more damage in a sense was done to the picture by the interference with the soundtrack than with the image itself. But

Eve: Stanley Baker, Virna Lisi, Jeanne Moreau

the film was damaged in a way very related to music, and very related to what we are talking about; because the cuts sometimes are of whole sequences, but more often than not they are chunks out of the middle of a shot or little trims at the ends of shots which totally destroy the lyricism of the film. If you are dealing with a subject which is harsh and cruel, and to many people repugnant as in the case of *Eve*, as in the case of *Accident*, *The Servant* or *King and Country*, and if you are going to handle it, as I have tried to, so that people can see what beauty is there, what anguish, and have compassion and some understanding, then rhythm of music and rhythm of cutting, and the relationship of one to the other as well as performances, is essential. And any interference with this is disastrous. If you are attempting to do something delicately balanced, *you* may lose your balance—one does; one may be very wrong—but if somebody else comes along and sets off a firecracker or cuts the rope, then there's very little left to be seen.

In a way, the "Black Leather" song in The Damned *is one of the most jarring uses of music in your work. It is virtually a repetition, underlining what has already been stated by the film.*

31

The Damned

Yes, well again . . . this is not in any sense an apology, I don't
mean to apologise but to explain, for people who are interested
enough in films to want to know if sometimes they don't go quite
the way they should; so people can understand that sometimes the
best effect achieved may be an accident, an accident arising out of
something which is true but none the less wasn't the intention; and
that some of the worst things come out of an accident, or the
combination of art and commerce, or the various other splits which
rule the film business-art. I undertook *The Damned*, from a novel
I thought confused and not very good, because several other
projects had fallen through at that moment, and it was a difficult
period in my life. This has never been sufficient reason for me to
take on anything; but I did, because I thought the novel spoke
passionately and felt passionately about the irresponsible use of the
new atomic powers put into the hands of the human race, and

about the lack of responsibility of scientists for what they create. I knew I was making it for a company distinguished for making pretty horrid horror films, and I knew they were primarily interested in the science-fiction aspects of *The Damned*. I, on the other hand, was interested in parallel levels of violence: the violence I saw in kids, the violence of rock'n'roll and leather-boys on motor cycles; the violence of the world everybody lives in, of the scientists, of the governments, of the nations, of the establishments, which has to accept some responsibility for the violence one saw then in the extreme young.

Richard MacDonald and I found the location—Weymouth, which was seedy-Victorian, and the astonishing landscape, bleak, marvellous, primitive and terrifying, of Portland Bill. These were the things I wanted to play on; the science-fiction aspects of the story didn't interest me at all. Evan Jones wrote the script as we went along, because there were the usual pressures of time and budget; and the story *is* faulty, the film *is* slightly disjointed, but I think it has passionate moments. I was probably over-interested by the contrast between the seedy Victoriana and the leather-boys on their motor-cycles. I was fascinated by Weymouth, which was a part of England I hadn't really seen: the old Victorian clock-tower falling to bits, the remnants of quite beautiful houses, the seediness, the utter horror of the beach and the shooting-galleries, then suddenly stuck up in the middle of the promenade that figure of George IV, recently repainted. These things do fascinate me, sometimes slightly without discipline, which is perhaps one of the reasons for the use of the word 'baroque' in a pejorative sense about my work. Also, at that time the rebellious young were mostly teddyboys, and I was very interested in the fact that they were making their rebellion through exaggerated distortions of Edwardian costumes, and so on. So I wanted to use the umbrella, for instance, and various other things which were not untrue but were exaggerations . . . the "Kill, Kill, Kill" song, perhaps, which certainly was a statement of something already stated. But it was not a very easy film in which to be subtle; in fact I don't think there is any subtlety in it, except around the sculpture, and the

The Damned: "The desolation of the end"

final scene with the sculptress and her statement. I also like very much the desolation of the end, moving away from the cave where the children are locked in and the cries for help, and then coming to the beach. The children were a bit 'theatrical children', which is something one is often stuck with here in England.

But very often in your middle-period films one finds this apparent desire to explain your theme, to state something which is inherent in the film: the rock number in The Damned *and the conversation about violence in the hotel. Even in* Eve, *the whole business of the ornamental eggs which litter Eve's apartment with their symbolism—isn't this almost a decoration of something already in the film?*

I think you're probably right, but I believe *Eve* was a turning-point, although it does suffer to some extent from what you're describing, primarily because of the whole battle of getting films done—and it *is* a battle all the time. In a curious way I believe

Eve: Stanley Baker ("What about this?") with egg

things are changing, and it is becoming slightly less of a battle. I
don't mean necessarily for me: actually the more things seem to
work for me, the less I seem to be able to get what I really want
done, because there is more pressure on me to do things I don't
want to do, and it also makes it much harder for me to wait.
In general, things are slowly changing, catastrophically slowly. But
because of the fight there is frequently over-compensation. One
does things which, left entirely to oneself, one wouldn't do. It isn't
just a child kicking over a sandcastle, it isn't just a childish protest;
it's that if you admit a tiny little bit of interference or compromise,
it's an opening wedge and the whole thing can fall to pieces.
Therefore one goes—I go—much further than one normally
would, over-stating in order to make a point against the sometimes
anonymous foes and depredators. Sometimes, too, you put in more
than you have to partly because of the critics, who don't understand. I've tried very hard not to do this since *Eve*, perhaps in a
sense beginning with *Eve*, but certainly since then. I think fairly

successfully. But then of course the opposite happens . . . the films are called not clear, ambiguous, and are misinterpreted or totally misunderstood.

As far as *Eve* is concerned, it was intended as some sort of statement about marriage, about middle-class marriage and about middle-class male-female relationships in a particular society. I removed it from the usual context so people might have a chance of seeing it with a bit of objectivity, without immediately applying it to themselves, hoping it might have some self-application on second thought or viewing. An essential thing was the lyricism and the poetry and the compassion—the intended compassion, anyway. The eggs started quite simply as a desire to find something which the woman would collect, because I wanted to present her as essentially a middle-class woman with a little middle-class nest, acquiring possessions the way the others do as a kind of security and comfort. Jeanne Moreau suggested eggs, and up to that time I had never seen any of these ornamental eggs—or if I had, I suppose I hadn't been aware of them; and when this was suggested to the producers they said nonsense, nobody has eggs. I then saw eggs every place I went, they really were every place I went. Partly because of the damn producers we went a great deal too far with them, there's no question about that. And then of course in terms of rationalising it, the egg was a perfect kind of symbol because I was trying to talk about the crossing of the sexes among other things, and about the stupid insistence on maleness or the difference between man and woman, and the egg was perfect because it is both a male and a female symbol. But it was too much: self-indulgent in the sense that I was saying, whether consciously or not, "Well, I'll show 'em." I also think that while Richard MacDonald and I work extremely well together and owe each other a great deal, there was then, probably less so now, a certain tendency to compound each other's intransigence because we feel the same way about things. On the other hand, if you could have seen the film as completed, you might have raised this point, but I don't think you would have been as aware of it.

Eve: Jeanne Moreau

I agree, and the completer version shown at the National Film Theatre is very different. But I wasn't referring only to the eggs. Eve is almost too rich in its symbols: the mirror images, the Biblical references, the mask in the night club scene.

Once again this is the history of film-making, or at least it's the history of my film-making. I had wanted to have a dance in the cabaret which was to be a dance about the ambivalence of sex, and for various reasons—producer reasons again, because they didn't understand what I was talking about—this got completely destroyed. There was a gifted Negro dancer I wanted to use, and I thought maybe with the mask I could get some of the comment I'd intended back into the dance. Whether it worked or not I don't really know . . . I don't think it did. Then when I got to the Venice scenes, I wanted to recall things so they would interrelate and I used the same mask . . . Venice being a city of masks, a city of façades, of carnival. If I were remaking the film I would, I'm sure, use these things differently or perhaps not use them at all. I tried to get more into *Eve* than should be put into one film; which was a form of desperation because it always seems as though it's a last chance which won't come again. I think I'm over this now, but I also feel very strongly in this connection that there isn't any reason why a good film shouldn't be viewable many times with additional value each time. In fact, there is every reason why it should.

Eve: Jeanne Moreau

2: Problems of Expression

The increasing density and complexity of your films is one of theme too, very different from the simplicity and naked statements of your early Hollywood films.

This past New Year's night I was on a somewhat disastrous television programme called "Look of the Year", and one of the men on the panel, Denis Potter, was talking about a book on the Spanish Civil War. "All you gentlemen belong to the Thirties," he said, "and I'm getting terribly tired of hearing about what a wonderful period it was, how easy life was and how simple the solutions were. . . . Look at you all now, you're just a bit shabbier." Which was a very good and very genuine statement, and one I would have wished to pursue for the whole evening; but it was cut off abruptly and not pursued at all.

The fact is that the people who were part of the protest in the Thirties—and I certainly include myself—were a bit simple-minded and highly romantic in spite of the Marxist-Materialist ideological orientation most of us had; and so we came up against a tough, realistic and adult world with a good deal of shock and rather late in life. When I began to make films in Hollywood, I had not only full confidence, but an absolute delight in stating issues I saw to be true, with perfect faith that they were soluble and that I could contribute to their solution. The world isn't so simple. And actually before I ever made a film, although I had moved along

On location for *The Dividing Line*

these lines in the theatre, on that fatal day which I remember even to the setting sun over the sea, at about 4.30 in the afternoon on the radio going down to my house on the beach in California, I heard of the death of Roosevelt. I think all of us had a sinking heart at that moment. I knew Roosevelt slightly, and had met him a few times over the years; I certainly didn't approve of everything he did, but he was an astonishing force in the whole world, and the whole era changed at that moment. And it changed further and drastically into a period to which no end has yet been found when the atom bomb was exploded a few months later, an atom bomb which Roosevelt had instigated. The question of whether he would have dropped it is one nobody will ever be able to answer. Anyway it was dropped, and the world changed; the spy mania about nuclear secrets sprang up; the un-American activities committee moved in, probably almost entirely to take advantage of Hollywood's publicity value; and the intellectual core of Hollywood disappeared virtually overnight. Within a few years any kind of really strong intellectual freedom of thought, let alone expression, disappeared in the United States.

So there are all sorts of reasons for not having confidence in oneself and in film companies which contributed to the quite illegal and never actually recognised blacklist, which was none the less quite real. I think we all became different human beings with different evaluations of what we thought, what we knew, how we worked, and we matured in other ways. If there is a talent—visual, theatrical, cinematic, poetic—in the Thirties, Forties, Fifties and even Sixties, it has to have some sort of social orientation; but it isn't so smug now or so simple. There aren't any ready-made answers, or easy answers, or any complete answers, and nobody, including parents to children, or teachers to students, or theologians to initiates—any such relationship—can provide answers for anybody else. You can only provide a stimulation which I think at its best is some sort of complete artistic statement, which therefore is form and emotion, which will stimulate the people seeing, hearing, absorbing it, to further thought and investigation. Which is why things certainly should have many different levels, and why many interpretations of films, if they're that good, are perfectly justified, even though they may not be fully intended by the creators or fully thought out by them.

*There has always been a resistance in England to what might be called your middle-period films—*Time Without Pity, *for instance. It is a resistance which covers other directors who made their first films in Hollywood around the same time as you, such as Aldrich and Fuller, whom people found hard to take and wrote off as 'hysterical'. Obviously one cannot simply dismiss films like* Kiss Me Deadly *or* Run of the Arrow *in this way, but they do share with* Time Without Pity *a tendency to over-statement which occasionally makes them overbalance into absurdity.*

I know what you mean, and I think you are right basically . . . this relates to what I have just been saying. We were making, or at least I was making, pretty direct statements in Hollywood, also developing somewhat as a technician, as a worker in the medium. Then there was an interruption, and continuity is terribly important to technical security as well as to many other things. Also there was a real persecution from which I suffered along with a lot of other people. This was a climate. And there was also a necessity for total reappraisal of what we had thought the world was like (or at least what I had: I don't know that I have the right to involve others, though I think there can be generalisations). Partly because of the typecasting nonsense in Hollywood, after my first film I had been cast in the role of a director of melodrama. So of course when I began to work again here, I was, in the case of *The Sleeping Tiger*, handed a piece of sensational melodrama which had no real premise and didn't hang together. In my desperation I probably started to load, a desperation not helped by the fact that I was working on a closed set, where I was not supposed to be directing the picture I was directing and everybody knew I was, and was being paid peanuts for—and was glad to do it, too.

By the time I got to *Time Without Pity*, which was the first film anybody here in Europe had the courage to let me put my name on,

The Sleeping Tiger

I was again dealing with a subject which was not a very good one. We had to turn it upside down to try to make it into something with 'something to say'. I think by this time I and others in my position were somewhat hysterical in our hammering out, no matter how small the point, and probably somewhat bitter too. As far as I'm concerned at least, this has since relaxed, and it relaxed partly through *Time Without Pity*, which was the first of my new films which got recognition in France. You'll find, by the way, most of them are pretty passionate in their belief in *Time Without Pity*; it is a film I haven't seen in a long time, and I doubt whether I'd agree with them if I did, but I don't know. I loved working with Leo McKern, and with some of the other actors. The subject was a phony subject; visually it was exciting. But there was, I think, another element: I was still a foreigner in England—I'm a foreigner

44

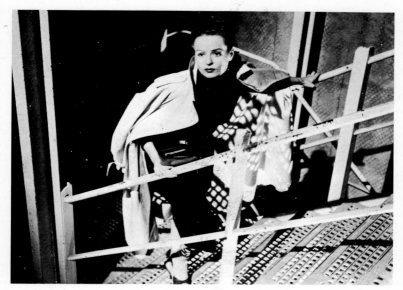

The Intimate Stranger: Mary Murphy

wherever I am and always will be—and my eye was foreign, seeing strange things which now would be quite ordinary to me.

After it—well, *The Gypsy and the Gentleman* came in between, and that's a bitter story I don't want to go into—quite a long time after it came *Blind Date*, which was the result of another bout of the blacklist as it affected me. I had planned to do a picture of much larger scope and subject, and was unable to because of fears of the blacklist, so it was channelled into *Blind Date*, which was a very ordinary script. Hardy Krüger and I and the two writers, Ben Barzman and Millard Lampell, had one month to find something in it to be interested in. We knew the story was a cliché, we knew that like most of these things it didn't quite hold water although the basic device was excellent; and we felt the only justification for this film was on the one hand skill and on the other to make the

Time Without Pity: a 'foreigner's' view

characters so interesting that it had a level other than mere suspense. It was fun to do, and was I think a good film as far as it goes. It also suffers from certain exaggerations.

For *The Criminal,* again the same thing. The original script was a hodge-podge of every American prison film ever made, absolutely horrible, not even written in terms of English speech idiom. I got Alun Owen, who had never written a film script, to work on it; and with some authentic documentation from prison workers and criminals, we got a script which had a great deal of point and was very real in its people and its speech, but which didn't hold together as well as it should structurally because we were forced to retain a melodramatic structure none of us was really interested in. But I think this is the beginning as far as work in Europe is concerned: maybe with *Blind Date*; maybe with *Time Without Pity*; but certainly with *The Criminal.* The characters were beginning to develop as real people; the films were not always totally defensible,

46

The Criminal: Stanley Baker

but the characters at least in my terms *were* defensible in one way or another, whether you accept the defence or not.

The Damned came into this category too in a way: the more subtle developments were in the sculptress and the Alexander Knox character, and perhaps the James Villiers character. But the real opportunity—or at least it seemed to be the opportunity—was *Eve*, and we have covered that story. By the time of *The Servant*, all these things had been brought to bear on me in one way or another, and on myself by myself, so there was no longer a desire to make direct statements, no longer a desire to give solutions, a greater security with the medium, a greater sense of knowledge of the society I was dealing with, and far greater freedom than I had ever had before. And also subjects of my choice. *The Servant, King and Country* and *Accident* were all scripts I wanted to do, and they were complete one way or another in themselves; they were entities, had their own style, from which one could develop a cinematic style.

In a way, summing up sociologically, one might almost say The Boy With Green Hair *is the last gasp of Thirties' social optimism, while by the end of your Hollywood period you are beginning to reflect McCarthyist depression and* angst. *Do you think this is something shared by directors like Aldrich and Fuller? Your films in the Fifties have a common denominator of real attack.*

I think in quite different ways it probably affected all of us. I can't speak about Fuller because I don't know his work. I believe he is the same person who was one of the many writers who worked with me on *The Living Newspaper*, but I have never seen him since then and I have never seen his work. As far as Aldrich is concerned, we were very closely associated in Hollywood: he was first assistant on two of my pictures before he became a director. We both came from very American backgrounds, his wealthy, mine not. We got on extremely well together, and we learned from each other a great deal. While he was never blacklisted, Bob was very much part of the struggle in Hollywood at the time it came up in the Directors Guild, and it had a considerable effect on him. I think he was and still is full of anger; he is a little younger than I, and as I say the things that made us were quite different, but the anger was the same. At one point we had planned to work together, and we were setting up a company in which we were both going to function as producer and director—I was going to produce for him, he for me, which would have been an extremely good arrangement. We had a number of subjects we wanted to do; one of them is still unmade, which I greatly regret; another he made as *Apache*, which was a script I was going to do originally. So there are of course similarities, but people react in different ways.

There is certainly a desire to attack in me and in Bob; it's a very real desire, a very vitalising desire; and I think it translates itself now into an inner violence rather than an exterior one. But at the time of *Time Without Pity*, I had been a long time without being able to say anything. That was 1956, and it was really the first film to have any sort of content after my last Hollywood ones in 1951. So it was at least five years of nothing. The subject was capital

49

Time Without Pity: Alec McCowen, Michael Redgrave →

punishment, and also attitudes towards sick people such as alcoholics, which had been treated in a different way in *M* and perhaps in *The Big Night*. It also happened to be the particular moment when the big fight about capital punishment was on in England. In fact the anti-capital punishment people didn't win then, though it looked as though they were about to—and I suppose all of my fury about the world as I saw it, the world as I was experiencing it, got into the film. It was almost the fury of an adolescent growing up. Because that was what it amounted to, although I was in what would be called middle-age then; my romanticism had to be reassessed rather considerably—or assessed, I don't know that I had ever assessed it.

So perhaps an inordinate amount of passion went into this particular subject. I felt—and I feel—that the killing of human beings, whether by the State in capital punishment, or by society in inquisitions, or by misunderstanding of diseased mentalities, or by war, whatever the forces, means that there is not really very much purpose in life unless these forces are understood, unless they are presented in some way so as to make them at least subject to examination by other people. Because of the repressions, perhaps the statements were exaggerated—I'm sure they were—and they were probably exaggerated also because they were out of any kind of context. By this I mean the vehicles were false, vehicles I was forced to accept. It was a question of what would be financed. *Time Without Pity* was based on a play by Emlyn Williams, a very good suspense play which had really nothing to say about capital punishment, to the extent that if I had anything to say, it said the reverse. But there were people who wanted to put money into it; and they didn't mind if it was stood on its head—or even know—provided it was *that* play, more or less. The same thing is true of all these early films: you have to have a core, so you start off with something you feel it's legitimate to talk about, and you go on from there.

In *Time Without Pity*, I was talking about men who are tyrants in their own families or in their businesses, about human beings who walk over other people to make fortunes, about people who

Time Without Pity: Joan Plowright, Michael Redgrave

go along with hypocrisies which they dress up in all sorts of trappings—not even the trappings are their own—and who are perhaps madmen, the kind of madmen who make wars, although not recognised as being mad, and who have totally disproportionate power over their sons, their wives, the society they live in. This was all part of it. It is also about father and son, about the condemnation of a man who was hopelessly sick as an alcoholic, and what makes him so, what makes him irresponsible. All these things contribute to a description of this film as what you have said many of my films are: overloaded, overpacked, overdense. But dense in a different way from *Accident*; dense in the sense of trying to say too much directly instead of through people and behaviour and . . . well, with less skill.

Of course the subject of Time Without Pity *remains a melodrama.*

Whatever you do to flesh it out in your own way, the shadow of the boy about to be hanged remains in the background. Perhaps the sense of unease one feels arises because, even though you have built your own complex relationships between the characters, the melodrama of the basic subject still shows through too strongly.

I think this is true. I try to avoid this problem to some extent by showing—as was not the case in the play—who the murderer was in a pre-credit sequence. So it wasn't a suspense story in the sense of who did it, though perhaps it was in the sense of will he get caught. Obviously it remains a melodrama, even with that suspense removed.

This avoidance of suspense is almost a regular practice with you, isn't it? In Eve *the relationship is revealed at the beginning; in* Blind Date *we know Hardy Krüger is innocent, and the Mexican boy in* The Dividing Line; *in* King and Country *the outcome is almost a fore-gone conclusion; and* The Big Night, *before it was re-edited, began with the last scene and then went into flashback.*

I don't know . . . I'd never really thought about it. I haven't seen *The Big Night* since I first came to England. It's the only picture I've had to leave unfinished, with the exception of *The Gypsy and the Gentleman*. I didn't *have* to leave *Gypsy*, but the score, sound-track and some editing had been imposed upon me, and I was so disaffected with the film that I didn't stay for the final work on the print and the mixing. With *The Big Night*, on the other hand, I had done the score and the mixing, but wasn't able to stay until there was a final print as I had a film to do in Italy. And while I was making the next film, I was blacklisted. The producer of *The Big Night*, who was young and inexperienced but perfectly decent, decided for reasons of his own that it should be told chrono-logically, whereas it had been planned in a frame of flashback like *Eve* and *Accident*. When I came to England about a year and a half later, I saw it for the first time in this form, was very disturbed by it, and have never seen it since. I can't say I remember it accurately

The Prowler: The 'melodramatic' denouement

enough to talk about it, but the producer now admits he made a very serious mistake. Yes . . . I hadn't thought about it before . . . but it was the same format. I suspect the reason is that I really don't want to make mystery stories or suspense stories; I don't *mind* making them, but not all the time. And after *The Dividing Line,* because of the melodrama which is what I like least about the film, every other picture I made in Hollywood, or was ever offered, was a melodrama. For me, the suspense must be not whether, but how.

Surely not The Prowler? *It isn't melodramatic in the sense that* Time Without Pity *is melodramatic—being based on certain unbelievable circumstances which contrive to lead to a desired end?*

The denouement is certainly melodramatic. I think *The Prowler* is quite a well-made picture, it's well put together and it overcomes a lot of inanities intrinsic to the story. But there is the same time element as in *Time Without Pity*, there is the question of the birth of the baby, and then new elements introduced such as possible knowledge of people as to when she got pregnant, and so on. In any case I believe the Italians call opera melodrama; and I suppose in a sense the thing these films of mine have in common—the thing most frequently objected to, and probably most pertinent to me until I grew out of or away from it—is the operatic aspect of the material, and if you like the arias, such as Leo McKern's performance . . .

Of course there is no reason why terms like melodrama—in the Italian sense—or baroque should necessarily be taken as derogatory. Your adumbrated version of Eve *would have been even more baroque than it is now, but it sounds wonderful none the less.*

There it was intended, but it may now be baroque in the wrong sense because of certain things I did—as I said earlier—almost out of protest. For instance, if left to myself, I would probably never have had Tyvian go to Venice in the morning coat in which he was dressed for the 'other' wedding. It was an idea, and when I presented it to the producers, they objected so strongly I became insistent about it, whereas left to my own devices I would probably have dropped it. But apart from a few such extravagances, I think *Eve* was a properly baroque film, because it was dealing with a baroque city, a baroque period, and essentially a baroque group of characters. It's the labelling that's troublesome—and this goes back to what we started with, the role and effect of critics, and different kinds of critics.

Their attitudes are perhaps understandable, because film critics are very often people not particularly interested in films; the daily critics in particular are people who have to do other jobs (although less frequently in England than in the U.S.); they may be theatre critics or even crime reporters during the day, or they may have started that way, or have drifted into film criticism because it's a sort of sinecure, not because they like it or know anything about it, or even *come* to know more about it. What standards is a critic going to use if in the same week or same day even, he has to review Godard, and Resnais, and let's say a *Carry On*? How can he? I don't think serious critics should be subjected to seeing the junk unless they want to be subjected to it: when I say 'the junk', you know what I mean—the average English product which caters to the lowest common denominator and which makes the English audience *have* a common denominator lower probably than any other audience in the world. It applies equally in America, where you find women approaching seventy who have reviewed films for the past thirty-five years, who wield an inordinate amount of power, and who still don't have any idea what they're seeing.

Because it is a commercial job, and because they have to consider distributors and also audiences, very often particular audiences, there is too a tendency on the part of critics to hedge and say "Well, I like it but probably you won't," or, "I think it's a marvellous film but I doubt if it will be commercial." By the very act of saying "I doubt if it will be commercial," they have already compromised its commercial possibilities . . . perhaps not with the audiences, because I don't think they read a review all the way through very often, but with the distributors, who say "You see? We said it wouldn't be commercial. He says it won't be commercial, we won't spend any more on advertising." The other question of comparisons and finding trends is absolutely legitimate if it is an examination of a serious piece of work in the context of a director's total output, or in the context of other films which may as a group have some relationship, because similar things happen in different parts of the world quite spontaneously and for quite different reasons. I often find that people are doing the same things I am, or I'm doing the same things they are, and I didn't know about it, they didn't know about it, and there's no question of imitation or influence at all. This is because we are all to some extent products of and influenced by what is going on around us in the world, no longer only in our particular country. This sort of criticism is quite legitimate, but as distinct from the cultists, from the trendy boys, from the opportunists and people who, like all too many exhibitors and backers, are not fundamentally interested in the cinema, know nothing about it historically, and have no wider horizon in the sense of understanding what goes into films or what the creators may contribute consciously or otherwise.

I myself am always learning, and one of the things I bitterly regret is that the only way you can learn is by doing. This is one of the penalties we all suffer from in this system. Of course, if you combine doing with talking and seeing and communication with colleagues, it is valuable, but essentially you have to *do* it to know. And there are problems—not just theoretical problems somebody else has explored or answered, because it can't be that way in the film medium—which have not been answered either theoretically or practically, and probably never will be answered except by each individual film-maker in so far as he arrives at his full possibilities.

Film has been described as a realistic medium. It is and it isn't. It's the most abstract medium in the world, and it's also the most realistic. It has a force no other medium has, excepting maybe television if it is dealing with a live subject. Sometimes there are certain contradictions between the immediate reality impact of the film medium and the conventions, the suspensions of credibility. One of the things which has troubled me most, for instance, is the question of language. I loathe and despise films where there are a variety of meaningless accents, or where people are supposed to switch from English to French or German and still go on speaking English. This is acceptable when the characters are speaking one language throughout, especially when it is a highly formal drama like, for instance, *Galileo*. I don't see any reason why *Galileo* shouldn't be made in English and set in a stylised but still fairly realistic Renaissance Italy; but this does not apply equally, as far as I am concerned, to *The Night of the Generals*, or to a story which has just been submitted to me about children in Vienna just after the last war where the characters would all have to be speaking English—because here the elements contradict each other. My own feeling is that I want to move further and further away from explorations of the culmination of this immediate reality impact into less directly realistic and less literal aspects of film. A few

The Boy With Green Hair: Dean Stockwell, Pat O'Brien

people are beginning to do this, but the explorations have hardly started. . . . Resnais is a pioneer, and in quite a different way, Godard also.

I had a letter recently from Ben Barzman, who was one of the co-authors of my first film, *The Boy With Green Hair,* which was made very nearly twenty years ago, had its difficulties, and wasn't widely seen. This year it was released for the first time in Paris, to remarkably favourable notices. Barzman says, "We were in Paris when *Green Hair* played and saw the reviews. Did you see the *Figaro Littéraire*? I've never seen such a review in my born days. What is it, they say, they built better than they knew." Now this is very gratifying, and it's nice the first film I made will be running simultaneously with *Accident.* But it's also slightly embarrassing, because I find the film unskilful and emotionally embarrassing on occasion. But apparently because of the context of what's going on in the world now it has some kind of emotional impact. Maybe people can find something in it which relates to what I'm doing now, and I'm not ashamed of it, but this whole question of realism in the medium is brought up by the film. The unrealistic scenes, like the one with the war orphans in the glade, and the posters in the gymnasium, I simply couldn't deal with. I had a bigger vision of those sequences than ever got on to the screen. If I had had around me people who understood a little more about what I was trying to say, I might have done better; if I had been experienced enough to say what I was trying to say a little more clearly, I might have done better. But I bogged down horribly in those scenes because there was this conflict in the use of the medium, and it wasn't solved or dealt with—or even recognised—either stylistically or technically.

One of the fantasy sequences which does work, though, is Pat O'Brien's song-and-dance scene with the King, played by Walter Catlett, which is both strange and charming, naïve in the right sense, and very unexpected in your work.

This was a delightful thing to do, because it was a set piece completely away from anything else in the film at that point, being entirely the child's fantasy of what the meeting would be like; and because I had two old vaudeville hams, marvellous and enchanting people, who did an act and delighted in doing it. It is in a way a forerunner of some of the things I tried to do in *Modesty Blaise*. I think I could do it much better now because I'd go much further.

The surprising thing is that this mood never crops up again in the film.

This is the fault. I should probably have used this style right the way through. Since the film was really dealing with a lonely child who suddenly found warmth in the fantasies spun by his grandfather out of his imagination and his past as a variety artiste, the child's vision of what was being described could have been absolutely marvellous; but I was working in a totally inflexible situation. Ironically, my whole film career has been quite different from anybody else's because *The Boy With Green Hair* cost over a million dollars, and until *Modesty Blaise* I never again made a picture costing so much.

It was an extraordinarily high budget for a variety of reasons. I myself got paid very little indeed, but Pat O'Brien, Robert Ryan, Barbara Hale and Dean Stockwell got enormously high money, so did several of the minor characters. We shot it in thirty-four days but it was Technicolor, which added 25 per cent to the budget; the "Nature Boy" song cost a whopping sum; and then there were studio overheads. They had three expensive writers, and two producers. For Technicolor at that time it was considered a very inexpensive picture, but not as films went and as my life went then. After it I was much more interested in working with freedom, and I did independent films, which had major backing occasionally and major distribution, but were not *their* films. We had marvellous crews, and we prided ourselves on working very fast and very efficiently. *The Prowler*, for instance, cost $700,000, and that included paying pretty big fees for the script and actors. Excepting *The Boy With Green Hair* and *Modesty Blaise*, no picture out of the eighteen I have now accomplished cost over a million dollars. *Modesty* cost three million, and was as high as that for many of the same reasons as *Boy With Green Hair*.

You have now made four films in colour, in all of which the colour is extremely good. To what extent is this due to work at the time of shooting, and to what extent to fuss at the laboratory?

It's due to both. In the case of *The Boy With Green Hair*, Adrian Scott—who was the first producer—and I both wanted to make it in 16 mm. As far as I know an important feature has never been shot in 16 mm and we didn't accomplish it. The main reason we wanted to do this was because the technical equipment for a moving camera was then much more flexible than in 35 mm, and also the lights needed were much more limited; and by keeping the

The Gypsy and the Gentleman

budget down we could have more freedom with the subject-matter. But more important than that, Eastman Colour, which was the 16 mm process then, was far better than Technicolor. But we couldn't get it, though we put up an enormous fight. Adrian unfortunately went off the film for blacklist reasons, and another producer came on who had an interest in Technicolor. But he was a man with whom I got along and we insisted on shooting without any of the then Technicolor rules—as much as we could in browns and greys and neutrals, and even blacks and whites, which was a new thing at the time.

On *The Gypsy and the Gentleman*, Richard MacDonald and I—also Ralph Brinton and Jack Hildyard—worked very hard ahead of time to make it look like Rowlandson prints, aiming at their kind of washed-out colour and staying away from the vivid picture-postcard colours of Technicolor. We had endless sessions with the

The Gypsy and the Gentleman: Flora Robson, June Laverick, Lyndon Brook

lab and enormous trouble on *Modesty Blaise*, which isn't precisely what I wanted in the way of colour. But it didn't matter so much as on *Accident*, because this was a flamboyant op-art affair. For me, some of the best colour in *Modesty* is in the Amsterdam sequences, where it isn't flamboyant at all. *Accident* I wanted to look almost like a non-colour film, excepting for the idyllic scenes, and even they were certainly not to be picture-postcard; also to stay away from the dreadful extreme blues and extreme yellows of Technicolor; and to be low-key, which has been a dirty word in colour for years.

On every film, from *The Boy With Green Hair* right through, it has meant a persistent and long, long struggle with the lab, with print stock, standardising of prints, lack of standards in projection, and a million other things: on *Accident* we went through seventeen prints before I would accept one—and got enormous cooperation.

Colour *is* marvellous if you can control it and then keep it. Something that is desperately needed—and I don't know why from a business point of view it hasn't happened—is a consistent international standard in relation to stock, lab, printing and even lights, in relation to colours. Much more than black-and-white, you get it and it's gone in the next print, which is absurd. Up till *Accident* I had said I don't ever want to make another colour film because it is too destroying: no matter how hard you work you don't get it, or if you do get it you don't keep it.

Modesty Blaise: Monica Vitti and op-art dungeon

3: Hollywood

I'd like to go back to The Boy With Green Hair *and your remarks about the weakness of the unrealistic elements. How exactly do you think the scenes in the glade and the gymnasium should have been done?*

Since *The Boy With Green Hair* has just opened in Paris to those pretty astonishing reviews, it becomes important to be rather more serious about it. Before talking about those scenes, I think it's probably also important to talk about the film. It was the first film I did in Hollywood, and it started with a very short story published in one of the Sunday supplements—the *New York Times*, I think. It was a highly mystical, even rather religious piece, which Dore Schary bought, and which always seemed to me to be—and maybe was even intended to be—basically an allegory about racism, not about peace, although peace, and green in relation to peace, was part of it. The original idea was to shoot it in 16 mm without stars, with an Irish music-hall artist in the part Pat O'Brien eventually played. This project began, was cancelled, and in the interval the un-American activities committee served their first subpoenas, among them one on my producer, Adrian Scott—who was one of the few producers ever served, and had quite properly been the white-headed boy of Hollywood, having done *Crossfire* and other remarkable films. This was the end of his career as a producer, and his life has been dogged by it ever since—unfortunately, because he was a quite brilliant contributive talent.

The film stopped, I did *Galileo*, I went to Washington with Brecht. After the Brecht hearings, at which Schary, at that time head of RKO and executive producer on *Boy With Green Hair*, took a very strong position and behaved marvellously, I saw Schary in New York. He had just come from the famous, now infamous, Waldorf Session. He said, "We'll do *Boy With Green Hair* some time." "After this, I don't believe it," I replied. But about a year later he rang to say it was going ahead, no longer with a non-name cast, not with the Irishman, Albert Sharpe, who was so extraordinary in *Finian's Rainbow*. Anyway, we began.

I was petrified. Schary, to my eternal gratitude, called me up to his office the day before we started shooting. I told him I was absolutely petrified and didn't know what I was doing. He said, "Look, whatever your opening shot is, take as long as you like, take all day if you like lining it up, or take half an hour, get it right as far as you can, or don't get it right, it doesn't matter. But when you shoot it, say 'Print' on the first take. I guarantee if it's not right we'll do it again. But if you print your first take on your first shot on your first picture, everyone will think you know what you're doing." I did just that, and he was right—it made an enormous difference to that picture and every other one I've made. I still do it sometimes when I don't know what I'm doing, it makes a quite incalculable difference to the morale of the crew. This is one of the great burdens of filming: you have all these people round you who are great in their own jobs and who have to believe you know what you are doing.

Anyhow, back to the fantasy. I worked with John Hubley, one of the founders of UPA—and later thrown out because of the blacklist, since when he has made his own incredible career (in spite of the blacklist) in advertising and in cartoons. Curiously enough, he had done practically the whole track and visuals of *Finian's Rainbow* as a cartoon before he was blacklisted. He worked with me as what was then known as a sketch artist—I'm eternally grateful to him, because there were many, many things I didn't know about camera and composition which he helped me with. In a way he was

The Boy With Green Hair: The gymnasium

a forerunner of Richard MacDonald, who became a mainstay of my method of working in this country.

My feeling was that this was a fantastic story based in reality but which had to have great fantasy. And I was stymied in both because the reality was the RKO lot, their clapboard houses and their

The Boy With Green Hair: The scene in the glade

streets which had been used a million times before; it's pretty hard
to get reality from that, so that was a problem. The trouble with the
fantasy was, nobody knew, nobody understood. What I wanted to
get, in the scene in the glade, was absolute horror, real terror, the
kind of thing Joris Ivens and John Ferno did in their film of the
Chinese-Japanese conflict, *The Four Hundred Million,* with that
shot of the baby sitting on the railway track, bombed and with no
clothes, desolate and crying. I wanted to get that kind of horror,
that kind of reality; I wanted to get the pellagra stomachs of the
Indian children, the dreadful starvation, the concentration-camp
feeling, into the glade. And I wanted to lead in to a completely
idyllic glade, absolute beauty into absolute horror. I wanted the
children all to be static and composed in ways that could be related
to the war posters in the gymnasium. I couldn't do it because it
needed John Hubley *to* do it: it really needed some degree of

69

animation, I think, as well as live shooting. It also needed active design, which he was not allowed to do because he worked with me only privately: they didn't admit this kind of function in the studio then. I also didn't know how to do it.

The other thing was they *built* the glade—and I remember this as a permanent lesson in my film life. I wanted to shoot the glade on location, but they said it would be much more expensive than shooting it in the studio. So they paid $9,000—this doesn't seem so much now, but it was twenty years ago—to bring in live trees to plant in the studio, building a cyclorama round, and planting the grass for the initial realism without any conception of what the anti-realism was going to be. It was one of two shots in the picture for which I asked for a big crane—this also was very expensive. And at that time Technicolor required—it still does, but more so then—an enormous amount of lighting and heat. My first shot, which I would now knock off in an hour or so, took the whole day, and I didn't get it. The next day we came on the set and the trees were all wilting, so they tied leaves on the trees. I had been given two days on the set, and I think we took four; by the end of the fourth day the trees were all dead and the set was unphotographable. I couldn't worry about style and what I didn't know. All this was a very good object lesson in how you cannot monkey with the film industry as industry in relation to art, unless you know what the economics are, and unless you know precisely what you are doing technically in trying to get a special effect. It didn't work in *Boy With Green Hair*: there's no horror and there's no reality in the glade, and the figures of the children are marionettes.

You didn't have any censorship on the film, then?

Oh, yes, I had censorship. I had worked and struggled through three or four years at M-G-M, where I shot practically no film. I had got to know Dore Schary, not through film-making but because I produced and directed two spectacles for him: one the Academy Award show at Grauman's Chinese Theatre in 1945 or 1946; and in 1945, two weeks after Roosevelt's death, the Roosevelt

Memorial Show at the Hollywood Bowl, which involved all sorts of incredible people—incredible to me then at any rate—like Ronald Colman and Charles Boyer. So we came to have a very great respect for each other. While I was at Metro we had discussed at great length what we wanted to do, and I was always taking things to Dore. Then he became head of RKO, and when he asked me to come and do *Boy With Green Hair* there, he said, "You'll have to sign a term contract, because that's the only way the company operates." I said I'd had it at Metro and wouldn't do it again, but he told me he'd just signed a five-year contract as production-chief at RKO, and there would be no problem if I also signed. So I said O.K., foolishly. Long before *Boy With Green Hair* was finished he was fired by Howard Hughes—fired in the sense of being bought out.

Adrian Scott was long since gone; my producer was a nice man but he had no idea what I was trying to get at; so on my first picture I was left alone to fight the ghost of Howard Hughes. Before he left, Dore had set up an advance advertising campaign which was extraordinary, so everybody knew about the film; and Hughes, whom I never met, was said not to have liked the sound of it. So Dore Schary's successor as head of RKO, a very nice man named Rathvon, called me into his vast, rather Mussolini office, and said, "Now look, what can we do about this film? Can't we change certain lines . . . can't we re-shoot?" But every day he brought pages of yellow paper—I realise as I'm telling this that it sounds like fiction, but it is literal fact—with scribbled notes in pencil about what to change. They came from Hughes's office. And every morning I sat and thought, "What am I going to do? I have nobody to help me, nobody knows what I'm talking about, how am I going to protect this picture?" I had to say, "This can't be done . . . that won't fit, etc.," without arguing content, because at that time peace was a dirty word, a really dirty word: you didn't talk about peace unless you were a Russian spy.

The only thing that probably saved *Boy With Green Hair* a little bit—saved it from my ignorance, my *naïveté*, and RKO—to a point where it can now be seriously considered at all, was that one day

I looked up from my anguish over the yellow papers across Mr Rathvon's desk—and he was pretty anguished too, he was a very decent man—to a picture on the wall, and said, "My God! Where did you get that picture?" It was a painting of Arab horsemen by Shierer, a nineteenth-century German romantic painter, and until I left my hometown of La Crosse, Wisconsin at the age of sixteen, I looked at it practically every day of my life because it hung on the stairway in my family's house. I was sure it was the same and asked him how he got it. He said, "Well, you know, when Paramount Theatres set up in their new and last phase, they bought a good deal of art at auction. Then when they went bankrupt, the pictures were going for sale. This was a picture I'd always loved and I was with Paramount, so I took it." The fact is that my family went bankrupt in rather romantic and incredible circumstances, and this picture was sold at auction in New York. Paramount bought it and hung it in the Brooklyn Paramount. . . . This established a certain *rapport* between us which made it possible for me to protect the intention of *Boy With Green Hair* to some degree. For instance, in the very naïve, very primitive and badly shot scene in the grocery store—where the boy drops a bottle of milk because he hears people talking about war—it was the intention and the wish of Howard Hughes to dub these lines so as to make the attacker the Russians. To some extent, but not very much, he succeeded. The picture is not precisely as I shot it; it's a very awkward film and I don't defend it, but its content was a great deal clearer before it was slightly corrupted.

But apart from these nibblings away, what you were trying to say was not affected?

Well, I quarrel very much with Dore Schary's concept of the basic subject. It was not an anti-war picture as a concept, as a device, it was anti-racist. The best scene in the film for me is the one in which the schoolteacher, after a certain amount of persecution of the boy by the children, asks how many of the children have black hair, how many have blond hair, how many have red hair—two hands—how many have green—one hand. This is the essence of the idea, this is what should have been done primarily, and it wasn't. The important thing to speak about then was peace. It's even more important now—hence, perhaps, the quite unrealistically good reviews in France where it is being seen for the first time.

In spite of what you say about the studio sets, the film seems to capture the atmosphere of a small town very well.

I don't think you would think so if you saw a small American town. I came from one, and it's quite different. That particular RKO small town set was used many times before and many times after; it was, of course, very well done because a great deal of money was spent on it, but it was *any* American small town, and any American small town is not like any other. It is much too generalised.

Would you say The Dividing Line *was much more specific?*

The Dividing Line was shot entirely on location, and far enough away from Hollywood so that all the extras are actual townspeople —even certain characters, sheriffs and such. I had two days studio on the picture, all the rest was location. Everything in the court-house, for instance, exterior and interior, is real. All the exteriors were in the town, and the whole town cooperated, from the mayor down.

Do you feel that, within its terms as one of your very early films, The Dividing Line *is satisfactory?*

The Dividing Line is the first film I made that I really liked. After *The Boy With Green Hair*, I still had some years of my term contract to go at RKO. Very shortly I was offered a film called

The Dividing Line: The Marysville location →

I Married a Communist, which I turned down categorically—I was the first. I later learned this was a touchstone for establishing who was not 'a red': you offered *I Married a Communist* to anybody you thought was a Communist, and if they turned it down, they were. It was turned down by thirteen directors before it was made, but in the meantime, somewhere before the thirteenth of us, round about the eighth or ninth in fact, it was offered to Nick Ray. He said yes, because he was on quite good terms with Howard Hughes, and thought he could get away with it. It was an incredible script, quite apart from the content. Nick was at that time in a much stronger position than I, having made a very successful film which Hughes liked, *They Live By Night*. He built the sets for *I Married a Communist*, worked on the script and rehearsed the actors, thinking nobody would ultimately make this idiotic picture. It came to about three or four days before shooting, when he realised they were going to do it and he would have to, so he walked out. I forget who finally did make the film, but it was a catastrophe.

As a result of this I was immobilised and out of work for a long, long time, and finally had to pay RKO to get out of my contract. I went back to New York, and Dore Schary then asked me to come to Metro as a scriptwriter, which I did. There I wrote in collaboration with several people a film for Lena Horne, whom I thought —and still think—is potentially a great actress. It was a serious dramatic film about the American Civil War. This was not coming about, and Dore asked me to work on something called *Murder at Harvard*, which I did. This wasn't coming about either. Then suddenly Pine and Thomas, a couple of independents working for Paramount, offered me a film written by Dan Mainwaring about the illegal Mexican immigrant workers. I liked it enormously, and told Dore I wasn't going to wait for *Murder at Harvard*. Dore has never really spoken to me since because he thought it was a breach of loyalty—in spite of the fact that in between I took him innumerable stories, many of which he made, not the least of which was a great story by Stephen Vincent Benét called "The Sobbin' Women", which became the musical *Seven Brides for Seven*

Brothers. I wanted to make it as a drama, and it would have been a great one, I think. Anyway, I left to do *The Dividing Line*.

Pine and Thomas were working for Paramount distribution at low cost, and the idea was to do everything as cheaply as possible. I didn't mind this, as I don't mind now. I agreed to an arrangement whereby twenty per cent of my fee was contingent upon my coming in under budget and under schedule, which I did and collected. Dan Mainwaring wrote a marvellous script, but there were unnecessary melodramatic elements in it which I detested and tried to eliminate, but couldn't. Such as the crash in the police car, and the so-called rape of the girl. I also objected strongly to the highly romanticised characters of the newspaper reporter and the Mexican girl whose father was the editor of the Mexican paper. This, at least as presented, was sheer nonsense. The Mexican workers in the fruit orchards, the so-called Aryan sons of the town, and the editor of the paper in the town itself, are I think very true. It was shot on location in Marysville and Grass Valley—actually Grass Valley is the town where Bret Harte and Robert Louis Stevenson lived during the days of the silver rush, and it's largely unknown. It was a joy to shoot there.

You once said that when the boy escapes across the loose stones while being hunted, you wanted the noise of his feet on the stones to be unnaturally, deafeningly loud and threatening. Was this the only time in the film you planned to use unrealistic sound?

I expect it was a beginning—after all, this was only my second film. Before this I had worked—and worked very happily and successfully—in radio; in fact I think some of my best work was done there. So I knew the importance of non-realistic exaggerated sound (either greater or lesser). That use of sound in *The Dividing Line* was suggested by the landscape I found at Grass Valley, which was the rubble of dredging for silver and gold. For miles and miles as far as you could see the countryside was laid waste, the arable land swept to the bottom of the river and the rocks pulled to the surface. Here you saw something you just couldn't

The Dividing Line

believe—a wilderness of rocks; and the sound of anybody being pursued across it was fantastic. There was no point in reproducing the sound literally, it had to be much bigger to create the full horror. But, obviously, I hadn't yet had the chance to understand the relationship of this kind of use of sound with film.

This is probably the first instance of your use of décor as a character, something you did much more successfully in your next film, The Prowler. *In fact, between* The Dividing Line *and* The Prowler *there seems to be an enormous leap forward in your assurance and awareness as a director.*

It is very difficult for me to look back and say what did what, and what produced what result. But for *The Dividing Line* the budget was $150,000; for *The Prowler*, $600,000 or $700,000. In the case of *The Dividing Line* I was working on a piecework basis, and I was dealing with people who, like Hammer Pictures, really wanted to turn out sensation but at the same time were looking for prestige cheap. My reputation for violence, which is in my own opinion completely without real basis, began on this picture; I did the job they asked me to do, and I did it within their terms all the time, but I was *always* frustrated—and I suppose this was my first experience of such frustration. So there was a considerable amount of violence, and it conditioned me to feel that producer and director interests were necessarily antagonistic.

The difference between *The Dividing Line* and *The Prowler* was that Sam Spiegel was a marvellous producer. His attitude was, "You're right for this, but you're not very experienced. I'll give you the best cameraman in Hollywood, the best technicians, the best first assistant. I don't care what I pay, and you do it any way you want to." This was extraordinary. I owe him a great deal, because I know nobody else in Hollywood at that time who could or would have given me that kind of freedom and implementation. As cameraman he gave me Arthur Miller, who never made a picture in under seventeen weeks, had been under contract to Fox for umpteen years, and had three Academy Awards; he gave me one of the best operators in the world, and he gave me Aldrich, God bless him; and he let me pre-rehearse.

It was on *The Prowler* that I learned one could really combine theatre and film: if you had actors you could dig into and produce something from, you could sustain their performances theatrically but in non-theatrical terms by or through camera movement. And Arthur Miller was delighted to do it because he wanted to prove he could—he'd never had the chance at Fox. In contrast to *The Dividing Line*, *The Prowler* was an absolute delight to do. I had one or two brief, violent ructions with Spiegel, and ultimately one disagreement with him over the length of a close-up—a matter of a few feet—and that's all. It was a totally different experience from Pine-Thomas, excepting for money. My fee was a third more than I got from them, and a great deal more than I earned in England for many years; but the last third I wasn't able to collect until three

The Spanish house in *The Prowler:* Evelyn Keyes and Van Heflin, with (above) John Maxwell.

or four years later, when it came in very handy as I was then in England, living off an occasional £75 earned by writing documentary scripts for the British Transport Commission.

How much pre-rehearsal did you have on The Prowler?

Two weeks. We pre-rehearsed and laid out the film with all the technicians present in a composite set. The sets which were not built—and there were very few—were laid out in chalk on a film stage, as in the theatre. Except for the locations, all of which were exteriors, every single bit of it was pre-rehearsed and recorded with the cameraman and everyone else before we began to shoot. Before this of course I had spent a great deal of time trying to find the right sort of horror for the Spanish house, and a great deal more with Hubley, reducing and particularising the horror. We shot it in twenty-one days, and it would have cost double if we hadn't rehearsed. At that time nobody would do this: but Spiegel understood. He didn't know much about me except that I had done two pictures, but he believed I would do it in the time I said I would if I had the rehearsal. This has become a pattern for me, and perhaps for many other people.

Was this the first time you had any pre-rehearsal at all?

I had some on *The Boy With Green Hair*, about three days on the set. It was a strange experience, because Pat O'Brien is a great old Hollywood star and hack—I use the word with endearment, because I think he is a marvellous actor, but he *was* what he was playing. On these three days of rehearsal, when I went through it with him on the set, he thought I was quite nuts. He didn't know any of his lines and he didn't know what the hell I was doing, but we became very great friends. On the first day he called me into his dressing-room where he had his own dresser—I was petrified of course, all this paraphernalia being quite new to me. At 8.30 in the morning he had half a tumblerful of Scotch in his hand, and he said, "Come on, what are the jokes, tell me the jokes." "What do you mean?" I said. "You've had the script for two weeks and we've been rehearsing for three days." But he just said, "The jokes . . . what are the lines, you tell me." But he did rehearse, and he was fairly impressed with the rehearsals. Van Heflin, Evelyn Keyes and the other actors in *The Prowler* were theatre-trained, at least partly, and they had a quite different attitude. Pat O'Brien came from the theatre, too, of course, but he'd been a long time in Hollywood.

The rehearsal certainly shows in The Prowler, *where the characters are much denser than in your earlier films. Perhaps this is why it seems so much more complex than* The Dividing Line.

I think so. *The Dividing Line* is very primitive as a piece of work, with one or two exceptions: the locations were effective, perhaps the kids, and I think poor, desperate, lonely, tragic Gail Russell's eyes counted for a great deal. But the film was further compromised by Pine and Thomas, who imposed on it a completely banal, anti-rhythmical score (against the rhythms of the picture, I mean), which effectively reduced it in all its sequences to what they thought the audience expected of those sequences.

In your next film, M, *you were obliged to follow the original script for reasons of censorship; but you are on record, I think, as saying you wanted to alter the whole conception because the Peter Kurten character in the original version is just a monster.*

This isn't quite accurate. I didn't say he was just a monster in the Lang version. I meant the attitude of the film-makers and of society then was that a sex maniac, or anyone guilty of sexual acts towards children, was a monster to be hounded down even by the criminal underworld—who were in fact his peers—because he was worse than they. This is obviously a pretty unenlightened and even old-fashioned view, and very few people would subscribe to it now. Most people realise that this sort of thing is a terrifying illness.

I didn't like the idea of doing a remake: I thought it was a brilliant piece of work on Lang's part, if you accepted this premise, which I couldn't then do, although I had accepted it along with everybody else when the Lang film first came out. It is and will remain a classic, which one doesn't want to compete with. So for a variety of reasons I somewhat reluctantly undertook my version. One was that there was a considerable Hollywood pinch because of political pressures, and I didn't want to go a long time without work. Another was that I was very much interested in David

Wayne, whom I thought brilliant and extraordinarily right for the part. And I undertook it with a restriction on the structure and basic story line, because the censorship office wouldn't pass it as a new script, only as a remake of a classic. Therefore my treatment of the central figure came into direct conflict with the whole structure; and in addition, the German/Austrian concept of the underworld in the late Twenties and early Thirties had nothing to do with any kind of equivalent in Los Angeles. So while a lot of that part of the film was interesting and fun to do, it just didn't fit, and might justifiably be called baroque and self-indulgent.

All that emerges from the film, really, is a couple of—I think—remarkable sequences, some previously unseen aspects of Los Angeles, and a fantastic performance from Wayne. It's a very flawed film: it contains some of my best work, but is certainly not a picture one can defend in any way excepting for its bits and pieces. A lot of people feel very strongly about it: some are very partisan, which I'm not; some resent it deeply because of its encroachment upon Lang. I believe Lang himself resented it, although I should be sorry if he did; I talked to him before I did it, and I think he was aware of the reasons. Others have said that it is a slavish copy, cut for cut, of the original, which is absolutely not true. I had seen Lang's picture soon after it came out in Munich in 1931, and saw it once more a few months before I shot my version, at which time the producer, who had also produced the original, ran it for me. I remembered from it one particular shot I thought couldn't be improved, which was the close-up of the maniac at the lock in the warehouse scene. That was the only consciously reproduced shot; I don't think any of the others were, and certainly not cut for cut. I didn't have access to a print for reference, excepting that one screening. And wouldn't have used it if I had.

My *M* hasn't been shown in many states in America—I don't know why, because I think it's probably a very valuable film socially. In fact it is still banned in quite a few states, and for that reason was a commercial failure. And throughout Europe, wherever it's been shown—if it has been shown—it has been terribly badly

M: David Wayne, Janine Perreau

censored. I saw it last in England shortly after I arrived: I hadn't been told it was censored, and I was horrified to find cuts—drastic cuts—right in the middle of long, sustained shots which had to be long and sustained to do justice to the quality of David Wayne's performance. The cuts which upset me most both came in scenes in which he appears alone or virtually alone. One was the scene in his bedroom which ends with him decapitating a plasticine figure: the whole middle was taken out, as well as the beginning. The other was his speech at the end, where he breaks down and incoherently reveals something of his insides and what made him what he was. Wayne gave an absolutely brilliant performance; the camera was completely static, and the shot as I remember ran over four and a half minutes, very close to five; and there was only one take. There were a lot of extras that day, and at the end of the take everybody burst into spontaneous applause—which I've never seen or heard before or since. This scene was absolutely savaged; and since there were no inter-cuts whatsoever, and no camera movement, it's just a great gap. Why, in God's name, was this done? There was nothing censorable: it was a man revealing his guts, but there's not a word, not a thought, that was censorable. I suppose in some places it may have been cut for reasons of length, which is equally stupid, but I was told the reasons were censorship. The complete version has never been shown here, at least not publicly, and I don't think it's been shown in France either.

I think the two versions are very different; but there is one other shot which looks as if it had been taken from Lang—the one of the crook popping up through the hole cut in the warehouse floor to find the police waiting for him.

I remember the shot, but not exactly how it was, and it certainly wasn't imitated. It is an exact situation out of the Lang version, there's no doubt about that—and there's really only one way you can shoot it. This was also one of the very few places in the Lang film where there is any humour at all, and I was trying to get humour, obviously, to relieve it. I would also say that *M* belongs

M: Luther Adler, David Wayne

to a period when I was loading things with symbols, sometimes rather heavy-handedly, sometimes for my own amusement, and sometimes without quite realising I was doing it. This is such a tricky business, because once people start thinking and talking of your work as being full of symbols, then they see symbols where there are none intended, and frequently miss the references which are intended. I don't know how you escape from that.

Oddly enough, though, your approach to the character often seems very similar to Lang's. His may be more objective, but both films arouse a good deal of sympathy for the child-murderer himself.

I don't think they were similar, really, although because of Peter Lorre, and undoubtedly because of Lang, the original character does arouse sympathy, you do feel he is a pathetic man and not just a monster. The whole structure of the Lang version (and this is what I was really trying to combat) is a melodrama, in which a group of pretty sordid characters pursue someone they and society consider to be lower and more dangerous than themselves. In structure it's a chase. I couldn't get away from that very much, but I tried to; and what little I could say about the character was done in terms of what I showed of his room and his behaviour when he was alone. I gave much more time to him.

The excellent scene with the bird in that strange, continental-style café, for instance: I don't recall that in the Lang version.

No, that was an invention of mine. I like that scene, and the introductory one when he is sitting on the bench alone. I also like one of the early scenes when he follows some children coming out of a bootblack's shop. Those were all original. There are of course other things very like the Lang film, not exactly copied, but they are there and they are essential. One of them is the image of the child's ball; another is the balloon floating away; but this was what I was shooting, this was the story.

M: Raymond Burr (right)

That café looks a little strange set down in the middle of a very concretely seen Los Angeles. Were you trying to compensate, to prepare a little for the European underworld atmosphere which would have to be brought in?

Yes, I was. And as well as sets, I tried to find some weird characters and actors who would play them that way: Martin Gabel who had never played in films before, Glenn Anders who is a much neglected actor as far as films go, and Luther Adler, who hadn't been seen much.

Of course this was my fourth film, and I was under considerable pressure then; this is not by way of apology, but I didn't know, and I don't know whether I'd know now, how to take something I had to adhere to in story line and situation and still make it different. It was a foolish thing to do, but the axe was falling all around me, I was sure it would fall on me shortly, and I had only done three films. I was at that point signing a contract to do three films for Stanley Kramer and Carl Foreman. I had brought several projects to them—*The Fourposter*, which I was to do, *High Noon*, which I was going to do with Foreman, and *The Wild One*. But however much they and I wanted these projects to go through, the contract was delayed and delayed by political pressures, as there seemed to be word around I would be hooked in next. So the lawyers presented me with a contract containing a clause that it could be cancelled if I were involved politically in any way, by the payment to me of a small cash sum. In the event there were delays in starting any pictures with me, the axe fell, and the contract was ended according to that clause. Since I knew this was going on—I didn't know what was going on politically, but I knew there was this doubt about the contract—and about a year had elapsed since shooting *The Prowler*, I felt I must do *M*, otherwise I might never make another film.

The atmosphere at the time of the witch hunting must have been terrifying. Is it something you want to talk about?

I don't mind. Yes . . . it was absolutely terrifying. You see, I began in Hollywood very late, and I wasn't really very much involved in what was going on there. This was the ironic part of it: I think my life in the Thirties was probably more reprehensible to the witch hunters than anything I did in Hollywood. But they weren't really interested in what happened before; they wanted the publicity of Hollywood. Anyway, you must remember on my very first picture, my very first producer, Adrian Scott, was taken off in the first lot before I'd even made the film. The film was stopped by the witch hunt, I felt very strongly about it, and I engaged very actively—probably this was part of what was against me—in combating it. I did a mass meeting for the first 'Nineteen' at the Shrine Auditorium, and I went to Washington later with Brecht, who was also among the first 'Nineteen'—was in fact the tenth, and the one who stopped the hearings for some years due to his astonishingly (to them) frank answers.

Then *Boy With Green Hair* was about to happen again; Dore Schary had testified, there was the Waldorf Conference, and *Boy With Green Hair* was again postponed. Finally I made the film, went on to *The Dividing Line, The Prowler, M* and *The Big Night*, and went to Europe. While I was on my first picture there I was blacklisted; in fact, *Stranger on the Prowl* was the first European picture made by Americans to be a casualty of the blacklist. It never appeared in its original form, all of the people who were in any way implicated in the witch hunts had their names taken off the credits, and the picture disappeared . . . and of course set me back enormously in many ways.

The pressure was an immediate, almost physical thing, from the moment I began on *Boy With Green Hair* until . . . oh, I suppose, five or six years ago. The most terrifying thing about the atmosphere was seeing people succumb, and seeing all protest disappear. Because if you did protest, you'd had it; if you were a university professor, or anybody, who dared to speak out, if you dared to say or do anything, it was the end. When I ultimately tried to track down the things I was supposedly nailed for, the reasons given were that I had gone to Marxist study groups (which indeed I had); that I had signed an *amicus curiae* brief along with hundreds of others for Adrian Scott (this was an official document going to the Supreme Court of the United States; it is a provision in the American Constitution, and is very much used); and that I, along with a thousand others, signed the peace appeal in 1948 or 1949. (When I say a thousand, there were hundreds of thousands, but there were an originating one thousand on the first petition. I was simply sent a card asking if I'd endorse it, which I did; I was not at any meeting—I don't say this with any pride; it just happens I wasn't even in the same city.) The last reason was I had been one of the sponsors of Hanns Eisler in the United States, which indeed I was—he was a friend and an extraordinary musician; but some other sponsors were Eleanor Roosevelt and the man who was then head of the New School of Social Research in New York. So you can see how all-embracing it was.

Undoubtedly there were many people who were not unjustly accused; but the point is the accusations should never have been made. And nobody ever, while asking "Are you a Communist, answer yes or no," bothered to define what a Communist was or to ask you what you thought. As Dalton Trumbo said, "Nobody has ever come to me with any real interest in finding out what my point of view is. Anybody who really wants to discuss my political or social point of view is welcome at any time and I will tell them. But I won't answer yes or no to a public inquisition." This is I think proper, and was the attitude of the people who stood up. But it became so terrifying . . . I know of suicides, deaths from heart attacks, talented writers who had to get jobs as waiters or in shops. Adrian Scott has never had his name on a picture since before *The Boy With Green Hair*. Marriages were destroyed, children destroyed . . . but the most serious thing was that the right of the American people to say what they thought with freedom and to protest against what they thought wrong, was destroyed. They lived, and still do to some extent, in an atmosphere of terror.

This is probably one of the reasons why the present generation is so nihilistic, because they don't really know what that fight was about, they don't really know what the hopes of the Thirties were, and there are now no organisations that are organs of protest. So the young are forming their own organisations to protest, but they are without theory and without orientation because they are essentially anarchistic. Hence, it seems to me anyway, all the things which came out of this atmosphere and the atom bomb—LSD and other contemporary manifestations. Strangely enough—and this is another irony of American history—it so often happens that the more liberal the government, the worse the reaction within the party when it begins to crumble or when there is a drastic change, as with the death of Roosevelt or the death of Kennedy (the Democratic Party is still the one elected by the progressive element in the United States). It was under Truman that these impositions began; it was under Truman, who was Roosevelt's vice-president, that the atom bomb was dropped and the Cold War began; it is under Johnson that the Vietnam war is being conducted.

Reading through the credits for your early films, one gets the impression of a constant stream of replacements for political reasons —Scott, Barzman, Ring Lardner, Trumbo. . . .

Yes, it was. Trumbo of course never actually got a credit. He wrote the original script of *The Prowler*, and went to jail while I was finishing the film. It was all a very incredible business. I remember going out with Spiegel to see Trumbo, who was enormously successful. He had been a baker, and he was a self-educated man of great talent who made incredible sums of money; he lived incredibly in a vast, incongruous place somewhere in the mountains outside Hollywood where he'd built his own trout lake and imported Italian marble and French antique furnishings. He himself worked in a tiny office piled to the ceiling with books and dictaphones and so forth. But when I began *The Prowler*, it couldn't be known he had written the original script, and he didn't either communicate or answer phone calls. So in order to discuss the script, Spiegel and I had to drive out one night to see him. The car had a blow-out in the wilderness, we didn't get to Trumbo's place till one or two in the morning, the conversations went on all night, and we left at dawn . . . and Trumbo's name never appeared in connection with the film. Trumbo is now making as much money or more as he ever did before, but as he said to me a few years ago in London, "All I have to do is deny I've written a script and its price goes up."

We have talked a little about The Big Night, *which I think I like better than you. Do you have any comments on it?*

I don't think there's much I can say about it—I don't remember it very well. It was the last film I made in Hollywood, on a low budget and in a very hurry-up way. I got the score recorded and did the soundtracks and the cut, but didn't stay for the final print.

The Big Night: John Barrymore Jnr., Howland Chamberlin, and (above) Preston Foster.

Then later, in England, I found the beginning had been transposed; it was told chronologically now, instead of being a long flashback, but otherwise the scenes weren't changed. I saw it for the first time around 1952, having made it in 1950, and was very disappointed: a great deal of it I felt was mawkish. I liked working with John Barrymore Jnr. enormously; he was difficult, untrained—when I say difficult, I mean it was hard to get him free—but enormously talented and a wasted man. I also thought Joan Lorring was an extremely gifted actress. It wasn't terribly well written; although my signature is on it and I was more actively involved in the writing than I've ever been before or since—or want to be—this was again partly a question of blacklist.

I do remember shooting the scene in the night club, which I was very pleased with: Dorothy Comingore is an enormously sensitive actress. Speaking of the blacklist, she reminds me of a terrifying story which may give you some idea of the atmosphere. I had seen her in *Citizen Kane*, but I didn't know her at all, had never even met her: I was never really part of Hollywood. All told, I was there for about seven years, I suppose, of which I was away for about three at various times. So I didn't really understand the blacklist thing, I didn't know who people were, what they had done or hadn't done. Anyway, I went to see Dorothy Comingore, and her hair was cut very short in close-cropped curls (I can't remember whether she used a wig in the film or left her hair as it was). When I saw her, I said, "My God! You had such a magnificent head of hair. Why did you cut it so short?" And she replied, "Well, I heard my husband on the radio testifying before the un-American activities committee and implicating his friends. I felt I was a collaborator, so I went out and had my head shaved."

4: Theatre and Cinema

Can we move even further back, and talk a little about your theatre activity and its relation to your work in the cinema? I think the main impression most people have is that you collaborated on The Living Newspaper: *this is obviously only part of the story.*

It's a large subject. It covers, after all, about sixteen years of my life. While it wasn't exactly a packed period—there were plenty of periods of unemployment as there always are in theatre or cinema —a good deal was done. *The Living Newspaper* covered one year (1936); I suppose it is better remembered than other things because it was the first of the Federal WPA subsidised theatres in the United States actually to produce anything, and it was also the one which had the greatest impact on critics and audiences, and the biggest influence on subsequent theatre. It was a very free time in the theatre, and very valuable to me as a formative experience—and for others in the cinema like Nick Ray, who worked with me as an actor.

I began with a period of writing occasional criticism for various theatre magazines, and fairly extensively in *Theatre Arts*. When I decided I really wanted to go into the theatre, which desire had, I suppose, been developing for many years but without recognition on my part, I became assistant stage manager with *Grand Hotel* for a year. After this I went on a tour of Europe, looking at theatre in various countries, and came back as stage manager with *Payment*

Deferred, which starred Charles Laughton. Laughton and I became very close friends and I was stage manager on his next production. This was a period of deadly depression in New York, with 16,000 unemployed registered members of Actors Equity. So the Federal Theatre was a great boon. Very quickly—I was twenty-three then —I managed to get some money and put together a production which gave Burgess Meredith a start to stardom. This was *Little Ol' Boy*, a play about a boys' reformatory which got extraordinary notices but didn't do very much business, and was the first of two plays I directed and co-produced with John Hammond, who is now a jazz impresario of international repute. The other was *Jayhawker*, a Civil War period play written in collaboration with Sinclair Lewis by Lloyd Lewis, who was a Chicago newspaperman and biographer of various Civil War figures. I did a semi-amateur, semi-professional production in Boston of *Gods of the Lightning*, an early Maxwell Anderson play about the Sacco and Vanzetti case which featured Norman Lloyd, whom I later brought down from Boston for *The Living Newspaper* and what was really his first chance in the professional theatre. And I directed *A Bride for the Unicorn*, a Denis Johnston play which I liked enormously, a highly stylised production for which Virgil Thompson wrote a largely vocal score.

Around this time I was doing a lot of what was then relatively experimental work. There was a new theatre coming up called the Theatre Union, which purported to be a working-class theatre and was largely supported by trade-union subscriptions; there was a group called the Civic Repertory Theatre, with whom I did a number of things, including Paul Green's long one-act play, *Hymn to the Rising Sun*, a poetic but cruel and frightening play about race problems and life on a Georgia chain gang, which started Charles Dingle on his way to the movies. I also did the first—in the United States, perhaps anywhere in the West— production in the round, of a play about the Spanish Civil War called *Who Fights This Battle?*, for which Paul Bowles, now known as a novelist, wrote a brilliant score.

I then went on to do a number of other plays, among them one about child labour, *Sunup to Sundown*. None of these productions were big commercial successes, and I think the most important aspect of my theatre work up to the time I went to Hollywood was its experimental nature, and perhaps also its political nature. During this time I was one of the directors of a political cabaret which held regular performances on Sunday afternoons, and which was the first—at that time, only—attempt to speak in cabaret form about topical things. There were one-act plays, sketches, and all forms of variety and entertainment were used to make clear a position of protest—a position *against* rather than any other kind of direct political position. During the war I also did a number of variety performances which were partly educational in intention, partly entertainment, called *The Lunch Hour Follies*; these were professional performances with top theatre people, presented to factory workers during their lunch breaks.

That, broadly speaking, was the concentrated theatre period until I went into radio. Then of course after going to Hollywood, but before I did *The Boy With Green Hair*, I did *Galileo* with Laughton, first in Hollywood with Brecht, and later in New York after Brecht had gone back to Germany. Before that, though, I went to New York to do a play called *The Great Campaign*, a play with music, highly stylised, and one of the first put on by ANTA [American National Theatre and Academy]. Then the theatre more or less disappeared from my life until England, where I did *The Wooden Dish* with Wilfrid Lawson, and later a play called *Night of the Ball* with Wendy Hiller and Gladys Cooper. To my great regret I haven't done any theatre since, because it's very hard to fit in with cinema; also because generally speaking the plays I would want to do aren't offered to me, since I am more active now in films. I tried desperately when I first arrived in England to get somebody to do *Galileo* and other Brecht plays; most of them have since been done, in my opinion rather badly, but at that time nobody was at all interested.

Could you elaborate on the experimental nature of your productions?

It's extremely difficult without going into the details of each

The Wooden Dish: Wilfrid Lawson with George Woodbridge and (behind) Joan Miller

production. But with the exception of *Little Ol' Boy, Jayhawker* and *Sunup to Sundown*, none of them were realistic, and all of them made some effort to break through the proscenium—something pretty well accepted now, but it wasn't then; and of course the cabaret and the *Lunch Hour Follies*, but particularly the Spanish Civil War play, were theatre in the round. *Who Fights This Battle?* was done on a central stage in a hotel ballroom, with no props except strictly functional ones which were carried on. The audience sat on the dance floor around a raised stage, and we used the aisles too. It was very exciting, and developed a new kind of actor-audience contact—new for New York—and a new kind of performance, because you had to worry about everything your body was doing, including your back. It gave me a great deal of freedom in staging; so did *The Living Newspaper*, where I had enormous facilities, including a vast corps of writers and researchers, a corps de ballet, and as many musicians as I wanted. They weren't always

The Wooden Dish: Wilfrid Lawson, Dorothy Bromiley

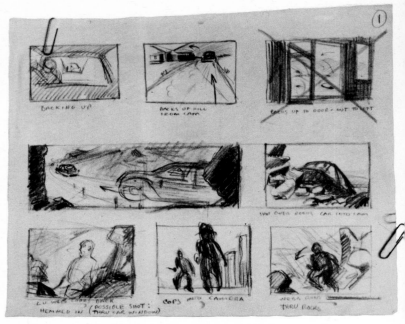

Preliminary sequence sketch by John Hubley for *The Prowler*

very good—the actors, in particular, were pretty bad—but the physical means were enormous. That one year was I suppose as valuable to me as all my other years in the theatre put together.

I forgot to mention, too, that at the beginning of the war I did a great many War Relief shows—United Nations, Russian War Relief—in fact I began them at the time the United States went to war. I did three or four at Madison Square Gardens, always with a central stage; I continued to do them even after I went into the army, including one for the last Roosevelt campaign; and I did similar shows in the Boston Arena, in Detroit, in Washington with Marian Anderson. These all used the same techniques—they were skits, they were educational, they were entertainment, attempting to combine dance, vaudeville, serious performance, direct statements, satire, comedy—but emotionally it was agitational theatre.

The Prowler

The Spanish Civil War play was also agitational to some extent, though it was a well-planned, poetic piece of writing: what it was saying was violent and emotional, because we were as deeply disturbed about the consequences which seemed bound to develop out of that war as people now are about Vietnam. All these things I'm speaking about are *towards* cinema in a way.

Something which fascinates most people is the way you like to work so closely with a designer—first Hubley, then MacDonald. Is this a carry-over from your theatre work?

In a curious way I think this is attributable in its beginnings to Brecht. When we seriously got down to contemplating rehearsals for *Galileo*, Brecht was anxious to impress upon me that his plays had humour, and were above all *theatrical* pieces. He felt that most English-speaking actors are set in one school and can only work that way. (Although I hadn't formulated it at that time, I felt this very strongly and had been working along these lines in a sense.) They haven't really got any freedom; they know little about either observation or improvisation; they are often insufficiently trained to express themselves in the medium of their choice; and they don't have enough range. Brecht wanted to give the comic dimension of the characters in *Galileo*, and particularly to show that they were *people* and not just cardboard figures, that for instance a Cardinal could be ridiculous. He also wanted to demonstrate theatrical groupings for a visual impact which might not relate simply to how the actors move around for a particular action.

This was another thing I began to learn from Brecht, and have since pushed much further than I did in my first work with him: he was very emphatic about, and taught me a great deal about *useless* movement. He said the thing which most irritated him about the English theatre was that you would look at an actor, drop your eyes for a moment to light a cigarette, and then look up again to find the actor somewhere else: useless movement, movement for no reason, which is just an empty kind of movement. And how much more effective the static is if it's *filled*. And also the use of many different methods and approaches, depending on what is useful and effective for a particular scene or a particular actor. Anyway, Brecht said the easiest way, he thought, to get through to a disparate group of actors the fact that they had to break their shells and begin to look a little more closely at what they were doing, was to get in a comic strip artist, a cartoonist. Hubley was the greatest of all American artists working in animated cartoon: I knew him, and I got him in. Hubley got the idea immediately, and he did extraordinary sketches for *Galileo*. Brecht was delighted with them, and so was I. These have been used in all of Brecht's own productions of *Galileo* since—in fact I think Brecht was more pleased with them than anything he'd ever had of the kind before or after.

When I first started in films it was really an extension of this which I began to work out with Hubley. Then when I came to England, I wanted this function, I looked for it, and I found it in Richard MacDonald, who at that time really didn't know anything about films. He hadn't worked in films or theatre, he had seen very few films, and hadn't really thought about cinema at all. He was an art teacher and an artist—which he still is. Our way of working developed over a period of years, and I think really is unique. Until *Accident* and until *Far From the Madding Crowd*, on which Richard worked with John Schlesinger, I've never worked without him in Europe and he's never worked without me. This, I suppose, is one way at least in which my theatre and film experience relate to each other.

A lot of people have asked what pre-design is (this is the name the French gave to the way I work). It isn't necessarily pre-design, because very often on a film there are no sketches at all, it is all simply worked out in talk; and on the drawing-board with practical building plans; on the stage with props; and then on the set where we decide what colours and other things we want. Sometimes there are set designs, but not very often. Sometimes there are continuity sketches, but very seldom, only perhaps if it's a sequence where I feel I'm going to be greatly pressured and don't want to forget anything or lose any step of it; or sometimes when it's simpler to convey intention to a cameraman or some other technician by showing sketches. More often than not Richard's sketches were not at all literal, but were sketches of character going back much more to the Hubley kind of cartoon. A number of sketches for *The Servant* are not even composed for a film frame. They are simply line drawings, and very beautiful ones, of the kind of thing I wanted to emanate from the characters—in this case to show the actors, but sometimes to show the cameraman or the costume people.

Sometimes there is a sketch which has no other purpose than to indicate a quality of lighting. Occasionally there are camera movements worked out in a diagrammatic way: I did more of this with Hubley than with Richard MacDonald, and progressively over the

Sketch by Richard MacDonald for the accident in *The Sleeping Tiger*

years I have been doing less and less. Sometimes, as in the case of *Modesty Blaise*, the things actually put to paper in the way of design may be nothing more than make-up details. For instance, all the op art in the villa was done on location by Richard and painted by him; while the rebuilding of the terraces, and the gardens were planned by him and by me with a gardener there. The Amsterdam flat was a real flat I found there, which we eventually reproduced exactly in the studio (even bringing a lot of the stuff from it) because we found we couldn't shoot in the real one except for a few interior to exterior shots. The bedroom where Willie Garvin has his affair with the girl was a real room—the scene was shot on location in Amsterdam—which looked just like that; I didn't change anything, I didn't bring in anything. The only set which was really a total invention as I recall was Willie Garvin's

Shooting the accident in *The Sleeping Tiger*

own room—I mean invention in the sense that we didn't shoot it on location or take it from anything, but just put it together.

And presumably Modesty's room at the beginning?

Quite right, yes. But it's simply . . . I suppose if I were a painter, if I had the gift of MacDonald or Hubley in line drawing, I probably wouldn't need this function at all. But the relationship does include another function which is terribly important to me, and which I have to find—or had to up till now—or thought I had to—with one person or another. I don't think there was anybody on *Accident*, so I don't suppose I do *have* to have it. But I always needed and wanted a sounding-board, somebody I could talk to, not to get ideas from necessarily, but just to hear my own ideas and as it were test them or reject them in the telling. Richard and I have a language worked out over many years which is partly drawn and partly verbal—very inarticulate verbal, at least on his part, but it works very well.

In a way, to sum up crudely, this pre-designing is almost a pin-pointing of useful movement?

Useful movement of actors, useful movement of camera. It is a process of selectivity, which I must say . . . I hate this business of "In what ways did Brecht influence you", "How much are you conscious of Brecht's influence" and so on—I think there was an interaction. Of course Brecht was a far more mature artist than I was at that time, of course he was a far more prolific and gifted man, but I think there was an interaction even between Brecht and me, and I think he learned a good many things, just as I did. Most of what I got from Brecht developed from a very brief experience with him into a much larger realisation on my part—perhaps this is what he intended at the time but I didn't fully understand . . . maybe, I don't know. Or maybe an extension. Textures, for instance. Something which Richard and I have always worked on and believed, and which I think perhaps came as much from us as it did from Brecht, is that if you're dealing on the screen with reality, if it is going to have any value as observation, it has to be a selective reality. So the first thing you do is throw everything away, throw everything out, remove every object, remove every décor, remove everything, and then begin to reconstruct it selectively in terms of the exact value of every prop, of every piece of architecture, of everything you are going to show. So there's no redundancy, no superfluity.

This may seem a contradiction of the famous 'baroque' label; but I don't think it is, because an object, one single object like a vase, for instance, can be baroque. I suppose it is really an attempt to perfect the visual aspect of a visual medium, also its auditory aspects, so as to show only the things you want to show for a specific effect or a specific purpose. Only in this way can one present on film anything more than what otherwise anybody could see for himself. This is the only way of making observation effective if it is in any way *illuminated* observation. It is also one of the hardest battles to win with cameramen and everybody else, and it is one of the reasons why I have had until recently such a violent objection to working in colour.

In colour you see a great deal more than you do in black and white, and until you have trained the people working with you, or unless you have vast time and money, the job of eliminating things you don't want to see but which are very conspicuous if lit in colour is terribly difficult. In *Modesty Blaise* I didn't like the colour because there was no selectivity at all on the part of the lighting cameraman about what he lit; so you would get an interior in the op art villa, for instance, where there wasn't *anything*. We were very careful to furnish the villa only with precisely the right number and quality of things we wanted in terms of textures and so on; but if you light that well and flat and with the great intensity which has been a technical requirement of Technicolor (otherwise they say, "Well, it isn't in the negative"), then you find that you're spending all your time in the lab trying to eliminate things you don't want to see and which you *cannot* eliminate from the set unless you eliminate them by the accents of your lighting. I did achieve this with Gerry Fisher on *Accident*, so some of my reticence about colour has disappeared. Most of it. But this question of textures, of getting the feel of things, of not having any object (whether it's a flower or a leather chair or a curtain) that doesn't have as well as its shape and its colour a texture you can visually sense—I suppose it's a way of making life as sharp and acute as one possibly can to all of the senses.

In Accident, *in terms of colour and texture, there seem to be three different textures: for the main body of the film, for the Francesca sequence, and for the scene in the television studio.*

I certainly meant to get something entirely different with the Francesca sequence, and the television studio scene probably goes

Accident: Delphine Seyrig, Dirk Bogarde →

Accident: Carole Caplin, Jacqueline Sassard

with the Francesca sequence, which immediately follows it. Those sequences, although obviously quite different in terms of what you see, are more related to each other in quality than they are to other parts of the film. Then I think there is another texture, and that is night and day. The overall texture of summer sunshine was very important, and very hard to get; and then the yellow of Oxford stone. On the interiors of the house, and also the colleges, the effort was primarily to remove colour, or at least colour that would be at all obtrusive; and at the same time to get cluttered interiors that were not purposeless, giving an overall sense of disorder. The texture of sunlight, I think, is probably one of the most important, not just sunlight, but sunlight coming and going, clouds moving, obscuring the sun and then revealing it, and the different ways things look when they're in the sun and when they're not, when they're in darkness or not. I don't like the exterior night scenes as well as I do other parts of the film: the blue and yellow lights used

Accident: Harold Pinter, Freddie Jones

for night lighting in colour are more obvious than they should have been. This was partly a question of time; we had great difficulty getting those night sequences, because we were running short of time on account of the weather. All those summer scenes were shot in icy cold weather, and a lot of it was in rain.

You certainly don't get that impression.

I know, but we would often prepare a shot for some hours and then get forty-five seconds to shoot it; and if it wasn't right on the first take, there wasn't time to do another; and by the time there seemed to be enough exposure to get another take, the sun had moved so completely that all the lights had to be changed. So it took days and days to get that stuff.

What exactly was your conception of the Francesca sequence, with its combination of very soft textures and dislocated sound?

Accident: Delphine Seyrig, Dirk Bogarde

This was a sequence which came largely from the book, where there was no direct dialogue, simply "he thought", "she thought", "he said you don't look a day older"—this sort of thing. The point of the scene was really that, as so often in this kind of situation, you find somebody with whom you have slept before because it's easier, because there are no responsibilities and no backlashes and you don't have to go through the agony of introduction or exploration or courtship; yet both people, being intelligent, must know you can't go back over anything which has been abandoned. So meeting Francesca was a kind of desperation on Stephen's part. He wasn't able to—didn't want to—announce his feelings about the girl, perhaps wasn't even fully aware of them; he had been frustrated in the television office; and he needed an outlet. Another man in that kind of situation would probably have found a prostitute.

Francesca, on the other hand, had the kind of life so many women do in big cities—makes a quite reasonable income, gets taken out to dinner a certain number of nights, and sleeps with a certain number of the people she dines with, usually old lovers who come around every so often; and she lives in the type of flat which I tried to place, around Bloomsbury, flats which are usually over dentists' offices or insurance offices in big Georgian houses, and which desperately cling to what is called 'taste' but are really completely impersonal. Stephen hasn't got much money, so he takes her out to a restaurant which perhaps she has suggested, where maybe he's never been before or maybe they remember from another time, vaguely Bohemian they think, where they're not likely to encounter anyone they know, and it gives them an illusion of going back ten years.

This scene, if it had been shot literally, with synchronised dialogue, would have been extremely dull, without pathos. Harold Pinter and I both felt that the conversation—which was banal, which was expected, which was if you like thought, but wasn't to be presented as thoughts—should be separated from the attempt at romance, the attempt to revive an affair, and be presented as a sort of abstract commentary by the people themselves. I think photographically the idea works extremely well, perhaps narratively too. But when I got into shooting it, my feeling was that it comprised two fantasies. His fantasy began when he heard her name mentioned in the television office, making him gallop to a memory and think "tonight will be exciting, to go back to that time ten years ago"; but it ended the moment he heard her voice, because of all the things that were wrong, all the things that had happened in between and were in her voice. For Francesca, not having expected a call, the fantasy begins when she hears his voice on the phone, and ends perhaps the moment she sees him. I think if we had consciously used the fantasy more elaborately, it might have been more baffling to some people, but it might have perhaps been a little better for the film. As it is, there is a slight confusion as to why the words aren't articulated, because they aren't too far removed from what is going on in the scene.

Another thing I only discovered at the last moment: again it's one of those things that happen on every film, and I don't imagine if I make films for another twenty years I'll ever get to the point where they don't happen, because they can't be anticipated, especially if you're conducting any sort of exploration. This happened partly because Delphine Seyrig was enormously busy and expensive and I got her to play the role on the basis of spending two days

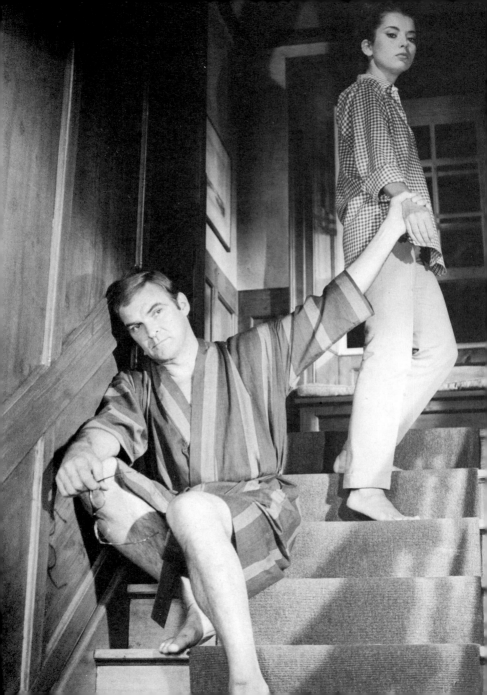

shooting in England. She came over on a Friday, we read and rehearsed, we shot the restaurant on Sunday, and the scene in the flat on Monday. Because there is no bath in English labs on Sunday nights, the first available bath was Monday, and she was gone before we saw rushes on Tuesday. I don't know if I'd have known until it was cut anyway, but . . . it's extraordinary how many times people make lip movements without any utterance whatever. It isn't noticeable if they are speaking, but if they are absolutely silent, you suddenly think they *are* speaking because there is a very definite lip movement, which may only be a self-conscious loosening or tightening of the mouth, or a clearing of the throat, or an "Ah!" Although both Delphine Seyrig and Dirk Bogarde knew they were not to speak and that their characters were not behaving in any way abnormally, they both make these lip movements. So I think there is a slight danger in the sequence that people will at first think it's out-of-synch; but I don't think it would ever have been possible to get the actors to eliminate all lip movement while acting with any kind of relaxation. So if I were doing it again, I would probably try to get a little further away from the actual reality as far as the speech is concerned.

Most people find this sequence particularly beautiful. It wasn't intended to be un-beautiful, but it certainly wasn't intended to be beautiful. The flat was meant to be cold and impersonal and slightly terrifying; the restaurant I deliberately filled with dirty colours—it's filled with colours but they're dirty—because it wasn't exactly elegant. The whole affair was not intended as a sort of glorification or dream, but as something pathetic and rather horrible; one of those things two people do, and neither of them speaks about, and will never do again; and if by any chance they meet again they will never refer to it. A real lost night, which instead of relieving frustration, makes it worse. So when Stephen then encounters immediately after it the girl with whom he has an undeclared affinity or passion, and who has been sleeping with his best friend in his house, the frustration is enormous; he wants to break things, wants to cry, wants to be vindictive, as he later is. But he is 'civilised', too. That really was the intention of the scene;

117

Accident: Stanley Baker, Jacqueline Sassard

Accident: Dirk Bogarde, Ann Firbank

it wasn't any attempt to be far out, but simply to begin to use the medium in a way which goes slightly beyond the absolutely literal.

This is also fairly obvious in the sequence which inter-cuts Stephen and his wife by the river-bank in the back yard of his mother-in-law's house, and the scene of watering the garden in the rain with Laura, wife of his best friend Charley, Charley having at least temporarily left her and the children, one of whom is seen in the window with a large cat. This, in a sense, is all collapsed in Stephen's mind. Rosalind is going to have a baby, Laura is at a point of desperation; he knows vaguely (whether it's defined or not) his own responsibility in this. Once again he speaks to his wife, confiding but not confiding, speaking about Francesca but not really telling, speaking about Anna and Charley but not really telling. Therefore no stunt was intended at all, but simply two duologues inter-cut in time and place; and at the end a deliberate sense that he is going to do—or is talking about doing—something he may already have done, which is part of his deception. If it seems a trick, then it's a failure; if it doesn't, then I think it's as much an extension of the medium as Picasso in his medium when he began to paint three or more aspects of the same face in one portrait. The fact is, when you look at somebody, if you are at all sensitive, you don't just see the full face, but the full face, profile, the good, the evil, and they're all collapsed or expanded into the same thing. Certainly it's far more difficult in film than in painting; but I think in a curious kind of way the throwing away of rules by directors like Lester and Godard is a step in the same direction, perhaps a little less politely, and maybe a little less successfully in the long run in terms of lasting result than Resnais, or Fellini, or maybe even me a little bit in *Accident*. But who can say? It's all along the same line.

5: Continuing Themes

More and more your recent films have tended to have what one might call a not-overt theme. A film like The Servant *can be explained in terms of social conflict and so forth, but it is difficult to sum up its theme concisely and precisely. The same is true of* Eve *and* Accident; *less so perhaps of* King *and* Country; *and* Modesty Blaise *is a rather special case. Are you moving away from direct subjects?*

In the first place, I am very much against the insistence on the idea that film is simply a narrative form. I'm not against it being used as a narrative form, but I don't want it to be limited to that, particularly since most people working in films are saddled with narrative by producers and distributors. Many of them feel there isn't any film unless, as they put it, there is a strong storyline. This is really nonsense, because there are very few basic plots; therefore the exploration of a plot, which is necessarily the same basically as many others, must be valuable only as a kind of framework on which you hang observation of all sorts of particular behaviour, general behaviour, and relationships, society in relation to individuals and so on. This also relates to the business of not offering solutions; but of course in the sense of what one *is* one is editorialising. Because while you are shaking somebody up to think, you are also in a sense pointing the way you want them to think, by the mere choice of what you want them to think about.

But I would say in connection with your question—yes, theme

On set for *King and Country*

rather than story, and beyond theme, which is not always any easier to make precise . . . I don't know, would you call it subject? Maybe I'm mystical about it . . . I don't intend to be, and I don't intend to take refuge in it, but I know that certainly Fellini, perhaps Resnais, Godard explicitly and Antonioni explicitly, all say they can't analyse their work, they don't know what they're doing, it emerges out of the filming. I think this is right, and progressively it happens more and more with me. After the fact you can go back and say, "This is about hypocrisy, this is about acceptance of

King and Country: Dirk Bogarde →

wrong values, this is about personal betrayal, this is about un-spoken conspiracy in human life"; but I prefer not to do that while I'm shooting, or until well after. And I'm not at all sure it isn't a danger to do it at any time.

I saw a review recently of a book of collected criticism by a young American woman, Susan Sontag. I haven't read the book, but in the review she was attacked for heading towards becoming a television explainer. This is a terrible danger if you are working creatively in any medium, and it's a thing painters and sculptors and even writers are not forced to do very much. Film-makers are pushed into doing it much more because of the necessity to make their films work, to prepare audiences and to prepare critics; and I think the need to explain does have an adverse effect on what you're doing. If I could do one film after another with a small, decent rest in between, and never answer any questions about what I had done or what I was going to do, I think my work would be a bit better. But it is a necessity, and when you are working in a medium which depends on money, not to do it is absurd. Even Antonioni has now been forced into doing it. . . .

A lot of critics, particularly in France, have been very reserved about King and Country. *Do you think this is because its theme, or apparent theme, is too simple? It ties up with what we were saying before about melodramatic plots: in this case there is a boy about to be shot, and one knows he will be shot, otherwise there is no film. Were you conscious of this?*

I was conscious of one thing about *King and Country*—I don't know to what extent it was conscious at the time, but at least partly—and this has been almost entirely missed by people who have liked or disliked the film. I set out to make a picture which, while set in World War I in a very specific and classically limited way, was to my own thinking *not* a war picture. As I have pointed out, no gun is fired in the entire picture excepting for the execution; there are no scenes of battle; and the only scenes of death and desolation are stills or static. Most people have taken it as a war film, and I have had innumerable letters saying this is the greatest war film ever made, and equally innumerable letters saying how dare I compete with *All Quiet on the Western Front*.

What I was really thinking of when I did *King and Country*—again, how explicitly I don't know—was the terrible situation every human being is trapped in, and progressively so in this century. Take that war, where millions of people went to the most hideous deaths, people of all classes, where they drowned in the mud, a quarter of a million of them, and others were left to die on the battlefield, others spent two, three or four years in inhuman conditions which eventually drove many of them totally mad and left many shellshocked for the rest of their lives—all over a tiny piece of land. It was a long frontier, a long battle line, but it didn't move forward or back by more than twenty or thirty miles.

This little man in the film, who simply couldn't stand it, who walked away and was caught, he doesn't believe in King and Country. He's fed this, and he says, "Well . . . King and Country!" But what's his alternative? Contempt in his community, an unhappy relationship with his wife, poverty, no kind of position. And the other man, the Colonel who is finally confronted with the situation, and who says, "I don't know"; or the Major played by Dirk Bogarde, who is at first very sure of his position and says shoot deserters like dogs, as you would a dog with a broken leg, but who in contact with this soldier comes to understand that it's not so simple. All these people, I think, are equally culpable, and equally trapped in different ways by the same thing. Because at a certain point they would have to admit, by instinct as in the case of the boy, by character and basic instinct, or by feelings and sympathy, as in the case of the Major, plus class and education, that the war is senseless, that they are not fighting for anything which means anything to them, and that the whole thing is an idiotic barbarity in relation to any of the civilisations we are born to and have to live our very finite lives in. So why are they doing it? Simply not to be shot as deserters, simply not to be thought of as contemptible conscientious objectors, simply, eventually, not to think any longer about the contradictions of society. All of these

King and Country: Jeremy Spenser (left)

people are culpable, including the young recruit, because the crisis brings them to the point of confronting each other, and not one of them takes an absolute position in relation to what he is or what he has come to understand. The men, the chorus—which is properly criticised as being slightly cardboard, but it had to be for various reasons—go further that way than others; and I think the Lieutenant played by James Villiers is a mouthpiece for a kind of attitude more admirable perhaps though less enlightened than those of either the Colonel or the Major.

To me, like *The Servant* and perhaps more acutely although in a more special situation, *King and Country* is a story about hypocrisy, a story about people who are brought up to a certain way of life, who are given the means to extend their knowledge and to extend their understanding, but are not given the opportunity to use their minds in connection with it, and who finally have to face

The Servant: James Fox, Sarah Miles, Dirk Bogarde

the fact that they have to be rebels in society, that they have to be outlaws and outcasts and outsiders in society for the rest of their lives, with all of the penalties this entails, or else they have to accept hypocrisy.

How many people in England honestly believe in God? And if you break that down to the educated intellectual population, what percentage actually believe in a personal God? What percentage believe in an impersonal God or force that is necessarily good? How many people go to church? And yet everything connected with our society is based on an assumption of belief—compulsory chapel, swearing on the Bible, "So Help Me God" on the part of every politician who is sworn in, the ritualistic observance of going to church on the part of presidents and prime ministers, who haven't been before and don't care. What about all these people who don't believe in it, who are paying for it, who still accept it? What about all these people who don't really believe in monarchy and are still paying for it? What about the vast majority of the world who don't believe in war in any form and are still permitting it? What about the man in the small house with the small income who wants a manservant and wants to live in a kind of pretence that it's still the same society it was in the nineteenth century? And what about the servant, who was a kind of gentleman's gentleman, but who no longer is a servant either, not in the sense all that tradition came from? They are all appurtenances, they are all encumbrances which damn few people have the will to reject—understandably, because life is very short and energy is shorter, and I dare say a different collection of appurtenances and hypocrisies occur in the existing socialist world. The alternative is to encourage people to be willing to make the desperate fight and take the desperate consequences of standing up as individuals, not saying "I can't take up a position on this because I don't know enough," but "I do take up a position because I just know it isn't true, it hasn't any function at all."

I think basically, if I have any one theme, it is this question of hypocrisy: the people who condemn others without looking at themselves, and the people with good educations and good minds

Eve: Jeanne Moreau's "Bloody Welshman!"

who accept, knowing they don't believe in it. It's the terrible business of intellectually recognising all kinds of things, reading the Sunday supplements, looking at television, going to movies, and saying yes, yes, it's so, isn't it terrible, and then going right back into one's little cage to act as though all these rules had some kind of legitimacy.

In the case of *Eve* I was trying to make some sort of comment on marriage, whether sanctified or unsanctified doesn't matter, any relationship between a man and a woman where each one supplies the maximum he can to the other, which in *Eve* I think Eve and Tyvian did. Whether this is easily understood by a large part of the audience I don't know, but to me Eve was giving Tyvian as much as she was capable of giving any man, other than the immediate pleasure, and he was giving her as much loyalty and everything else as he was capable of giving. And so, for me, this is a marriage. But it is none the less a destructive relationship, with something else, with some kind of comfort in it. The last line of *my* script—the one the Hakims wouldn't let me shoot, and the only line even Moreau was against—illustrates where you come up against these absolute barriers of hypocrisy and self-deception. In the final scene of the film, Eve is about to go off with the Greek, she has dismissed Tyvian, and he starts off across San Marco, saying, "In the bar of the Danieli when you get back." She says, "If I get back." As he leaves, she turns and says under her breath, "Bloody Welshman!" What I wanted was for her, after he had gone a certain distance, to call after him and say, "And don't forget to feed the cat." Because I think it's that kind of relationship, and I wanted to bring it home that it was to be viewed in the context of (as in Sherwood Anderson's title) Many Marriages—not *all*, but *many* marriages. The Hakims rejected the line, and so did Jeanne Moreau, because she didn't understand it. If the Hakims hadn't resisted so much, then I wouldn't have had trouble with her; but I couldn't fight them both, and she was on my side about everything else.

It is a marvellous end line, and one which would have made it quite clear what you were getting at. I wonder, though, if it might not have led the film back to that other accusation we were talking about —over-explanation.

It's always a terrible danger, and this is one of the conversations I have been having recurrently over the past eight months with Tennessee Williams while working on a script of his. He was rather stunned by seeing *Accident* because he didn't understand it; and I've been fighting with him—fighting in the nicest way, because we have no difficulties between us—getting him to cut more and more. I have cut forty pages out of the script; but until we do it at least, I can't get him to cut much more because he is a dealer in words, he doesn't know what the image conveys, and he hasn't any confidence in the image. I suggested replacing a three or four line speech by one word—all that was necessary—and he said, "Will they understand?" This attitude belongs to a school, a very literate and expressive school, which tells the audience everything. I don't think audiences *have* to be told that way; and if they are, it gets in the way of real experience. If the words themselves are an experience, that's another matter; and many of Tennessee Williams's words *are* an experience. What I'm talking about are the little things put in to take care of the fact that the audience is sure they know what you mean.

The Servant is most frequently criticised for its ending. Is this perhaps because what you once called the re-telling of the Faust theme comes in a little too overtly, and a little unprepared, at the end in the orgy sequence and the last scene between Barrett and Susan? Maybe it is simply that you can never really be open enough about depravity, but at the end one feels one has switched courses: in the earlier scenes, Barrett gains the upper hand convincingly in almost naturalistic terms as a servant, whereas at the end he becomes too open a Mephistopheles.

A lot has been said about the end of *The Servant*; I have said a lot about it, and you in your question said, "what you once called the Faust theme". . . . When *The Servant* was making its first very shaky appearance, I was asked, "What's it about?" by all the people who didn't know what they were going to do with it. Finally, in despair, I said "It's about Faust." This was a terrible over-simplification; it was something I hadn't thought of before; and it now comes back to belabour me all the time . . . because I can't defend it as being about Faust . . . I think I also said it's about Dorian Gray . . . it's about a dozen things . . . which is in line with my thinking that there are classic stories which will re-tell in different ways, and that there are elements of many stories in any one story. I couldn't then, and I can't now, say precisely what *The Servant* is about. The terror of speaking is that someone will come up with what you said, and you don't remember when you said it, *if* you said it, whether it is quoted properly, in what context. For instance, in a new book of criticism by an important French critic there is a chapter devoted to *The Servant*. It's a very intelligent and interesting piece of writing, very favourable both to me and to *The Servant*, so I shouldn't be carping, but he premises it on something he quotes me as having said, and which I know I never said. It is close enough for me to know what I *did* say, though I don't remember when or where. What he has quoted is

The Servant: Bogarde, Fox, Hazel Terry, Wendy Craig →

The Servant: Dirk Bogarde, James Fox

something I know I could never have said, so the whole premise is wrong.

In so far as I know my intention, the intention in *The Servant* was completely to reverse the roles at a certain point in the film. I think this reversal is correct. In addition to this reversal, and partly because of it, the whole style of the film changes; not necessarily the visual style, but the tempo, the degree of reality, the degree of extension of reality, and the morass of nightmare. All this, I think, was largely subjective. Harold Pinter had written a very specific orgy, not specific in relation to particular acts, but naked and with all sorts of suggestive background action glimpsed. There is really nothing so boring as an orgy—I haven't participated but I imagine so—and I'm sure there is nothing so unpornographic as an orgy to see, although it can be highly commercial as Antonioni has demonstrated in *Blow-Up*. What is suggested has far more

The Servant: The dope scene

impact than what is explicit, so the orgy in *The Servant* became a very English one in which nothing really happens. I also wanted to make it very clear at the end that this was a kind of *ménage à trois,* that there were all sorts of crossing of sex and not just homosexual implications; and that it was a story of the destruction not only of the master but of the servant.

Many people have said the film goes to pieces at this point, maybe because they think it's not credible. Many have said, "Couldn't you end it here . . . or there?" And of course, as with *Accident* and many of my films, you can end it in several different places. But I didn't, and if I had, it would have been a different film. You show a finished film to an audience, and they either like it or they don't; suggesting different endings is an exercise in critical semantics. I ended it the way I thought it should end, after struggling a long time over it; also, with camera movement, with completions of character patterns as I saw them, with completions of enclosures, it was necessary. I think there are certain weaknesses in the end of the film, but I wouldn't say they are in the so-called orgy. They are in the final scene between Tony and Susan before the orgy really begins; and perhaps, although it's extremely well played, the dope scene between Tony and Barrett. The reason these scenes don't quite work is probably because they are entirely sustained visually, and yet are too explicit as to both dialogue and visuals. Personally I *like* the orgy scene; I like the film, and I couldn't have made it any other way at the time. Nor do I think I would make it differently if I had to make it now . . . but I probably couldn't make it now. To each film its time.

I'm inclined to agree with you: in itself, the orgy is an excellent scene. Let me try to re-define what I'm saying. I don't object to the Faust idea, because the first part of the film could very well be a subtle re-telling of the legend. But it is, loosely speaking, around the orgy that the film seems to relax its grip on me. Is it that here Barrett's motivation is too explicit, whereas it wasn't before? Earlier Barrett was 'moving in' on the master, later pandering to him in the dope and orgy business; but in his viciousness in the last scene with Susan, in the way he is shot, he has become purely diabolical, he is evil, and he knows it.

Evil and Good are words I find difficult. I don't believe in absolutes. I believe in the existence of good and evil, but not in their existence in absolute forms. I think this is a picture of mutual disintegration, for the same reasons; and whether you reverse it, turn it upside-down or not, doesn't matter. The story could be told absolutely straight, as it was in the novel and the play; I didn't want that, neither did Harold Pinter. There isn't any strict reality in the whole picture; actually, the scenes in the restaurant, which were written during shooting, were put in because I felt there was a necessity to tie, stylistically, the scene in the country house (which is certainly not real, though based on reality) to the end scene of the orgy, which I knew was going to be stylistically different from the rest. All of this was the squeezing of drama, making it sharp in ways that are inescapable, intensification for purposes of communication of a reality to an audience. For me, two of the best scenes are the games—the ball on the stairs and the hide-and-seek—and there was another strange scene in the dining-room which was removed and which I now regret. The film was originally about twenty minutes longer. Everyone was terrified of it from the distribution angle, and I thought maybe it's difficult, maybe it's too long, maybe it shouldn't run over two hours—so I cut twenty minutes out of it. I learned long ago—and should have known then—that you never shorten a film or increase its pace by cutting, if it has been shot a certain way. But this was entirely my own decision, whatever the pressures may have been.

All from the last part?

No, three scenes from the first part, and then the longer scene in the dining-room.

Possibly the descent, the disintegration in the house is too abrupt after the very careful build-up of the first half; one's dissatisfaction, in fact, is simply that there is a stage missing.

I think that's right. I would really like to restore all the scenes which were cut. They do still exist.

What exactly are the missing scenes?

In the first part there was a scene between Barrett and his land-lady, very well played, in which he tells her he is leaving, and you realise they have had a rather strange sexual relationship. (This is after he has been interviewed for the job.) There was also in the first part a scene in which you see Susan and Tony meeting for the first time in a pub (the same pub where Tony and Barrett later meet) in the evening, round the coal fire when the pub is crowded: various class things were brought out, and a certain warmth between them. This ends with the two of them very close in front of the fire, which was the transition to the electric fire in the empty

The Servant: The transition after the cut pub scene

house, with the two of them on the floor. Then there is a scene shot in extreme but I think not evident slow motion, without words, in which the master is asleep over his tea, the maid comes in and fixes the flowers, and you realise he is not asleep and she knows it: the beginnings of the seduction. Then in the last part, immediately after the scene when Tony comes back from the pub, there is a dinner scene in which the master cooks and serves the dinner: this is the first time you see the house really transformed and the complete reversal. The scene was completely double-meaning: it's all chat, but chat about the army while they sit together at dinner. I like all these scenes, and I think they work well.

In the scene just before the end, Susan slaps Barrett's face as she leaves: what exactly did you mean to convey here, particularly in the context of what Susan's social status is supposed to be?

The Servant: The cut scene in the pub

Susan's exact social status, unfortunately, is very obscure in the film, and I think this is the film's chief weakness. It is very hard indeed, strangely enough, to find in England either men or women who have the background to play genuinely upper-class characters and who can also act. Oddly enough, in *The Servant* the upper-class girl is Sarah Miles; but she, for obvious reasons, couldn't play the other girl, nor could Wendy Craig have switched roles. I like Wendy Craig as an actress enormously, I like her personally, and after much searching I gave her the part. When we began shooting, I asked her to try to assume an upper-class manner and accent; and it was utterly hopeless . . . she became false and fraudulent and bad. So immediately I told her to play it in her own accent, which is basically Manchester. As soon as this happened, I had to find ways of justifying the relationship which are not for the most part in the text. She was, I assumed and suggest, an executive in an advertising office; she came from a middle-class family where she probably got a much better education than Tony did; she had a certain sense of humour about what was going on, so she could send it up; but she was in love with him. But it didn't work, because it wasn't an idea that preceded the shooting, and it wasn't in the script. Ideally that girl should have been entirely believable as of upper-class background.

As to her role in the orgy—and this was me, not Harold Pinter, because the whole orgy scene has about three lines of dialogue in it, the rest being invention to some extent as we went along—I felt that having gone as far as she had, and feeling as she did about this boy, and knowing as much as she did about him, and seeing what she did—which must have profoundly shocked her—she didn't fully know what she was going to do, but having been greatly humiliated wanted to do two things: she wanted to abase herself as much as he had abased himself, so they could have a meeting ground; and she wanted to challenge him by abasing herself so as to rouse him out of his own abasement. And of course neither happened so far as he was concerned, so it was a victory for the servant. At the door . . . I think this is maybe a slight catering to the general, if you like; the blow is to give the audience what I

think they all want, and I tried to make it as brutal as I could! Of course if she had been what is horrifyingly called in this country 'a lady', she would never have found herself in this position, nor would she have had to slap him, nor would she have had any of the other humiliations, because she would only have had to produce a certain accent and a certain attitude to reduce Barrett. But she couldn't, and this is why she in a sense gets on to his own level.

Perhaps it is a pity you didn't simply establish Susan as middle class.

If I had fully realised all the problems before I began shooting, I probably would have. I would like to add, though, that I think Wendy Craig is superb in the film. When *The Servant* came out, she was made to carry the burden of this particular failure, and it's not her fault. It's my fault, and Harold Pinter's, since we didn't have enough foresight—or time—to accommodate to it.

People have said you are a director without humour. I think this was disproved by The Servant, *but it has cropped up again over* Modesty Blaise.

I'm not a great party performer, nor am I a great raconteur, nor am I particularly interested in these gifts. I adore comedy or farce when it's very good, but my standards are high. Yes . . . I have heard I am both personally humourless and professionally humourless, and know nothing about comedy timing. I would hope any number of things in any number of my films disprove this. I have never had the opportunity to make a straight comedy—mind you, I haven't searched for it, but this type-casting makes it difficult even if you are searching. In my early days I worked in variety, or vaudeville as it was called in the United States, and in cabarets and stylised theatre where humour was essential; but it was perhaps more esoteric than what is considered humour in the film industry, where you are supposed to laugh at a daisy up your rear. It seems to me there is a great deal of humour, visual and otherwise,

Modesty Blaise: Monica Vitti

perhaps more visual than otherwise, in *The Servant, Accident, Modesty Blaise*, even *King and Country*; some in *The Damned*, a lot in *Eve*, a little in *The Prowler*, a little but without experience in *Boy With Green Hair*. That's at random, but no, I don't think I'm without humour.

Take, for instance, the scene in *Eve* where Stanley Baker is showing this woman whom he thinks of as a high-priced call-girl the usual tourist sights of Rome, and shows her Saint Peter's as seen through the keyhole of a monastery; she leads him on about her horrendous past, the classical past of a prostitute, extreme poverty, brutalised by a man at the age of eleven, and so on; which he takes absolutely straight, until she finally laughs and says, "You'd believe anything." This scene always delights me, but maybe it's too close for most people to laugh at or understand. Of course there are things I would like to have far more experience in, and which Dick Lester would probably do much better; but then for various reasons Lester at present knows this kind of thing better than I do, and would have more facilities, not necessarily facility, for it (more equipment, I mean, other than personal equipment). For instance, the chase scene in *Modesty* where three men pursuing a girl run into each other and knock each other out in an intended burlesque of, and comment on, Mack Sennett. It was maybe a little heavy: but if I can do it often enough, it won't be.

Modesty Blaise is probably the most controversial of your recent films, the most frequent comment being that it is "just a fun picture". What is your own view?

I don't think the attack on it as being a fun picture is a bad one, not that it would hurt either me or the picture. Unfortunately a large section of the audience that wants fun doesn't find it fun. I was talking to the distributor the other day, and he said there was a pre-sold market for the comic strip, and this was what they wanted. Also, audiences are pre-conditioned to a certain genre, and it was, I think, Antonioni who said in a *New York Times* interview that it was absurd to take an established genre and make fun of it.

But I wasn't making fun of the genre; I was using it and commenting on it—or at least that was the intention. And commenting with fun, with bitterness, with all of the equipment offered by the genre.

I made a mistake at Cannes, where there was a dreadful press conference and a dreadful showing of the film, and somebody asked the question which has been asked a million times since, "Why did you make *Modesty Blaise*?" One gets impatient with questions of this sort having just finished a picture, and I replied, "To make the James Bond to end James Bond." Of course I didn't really mean this, because *Modesty* isn't a James Bond, it was never intended to be, and I had no interest in either ending or perpetuating the series. I wanted to make a film full of fun, full of laughter of various kinds and at various levels, which would at the same time make the amorality of the James Bond films—and also, if I may say so, their occasional inadequacy as film-making—apparent. But since the film was advertised as a female James Bond, under the slogan (before the picture of that title) "Deadlier Than the Male", I couldn't fight.

One group thought I shouldn't have made the film at all; another thought why did I violate the genre; others said they couldn't understand it; and a few—not a few: it's on its way to grossing six million dollars—loved it, mainly people who have never heard of me. Zanuck, I must say, adored the film, and I liked working with him; he was very helpful and very professional. And so was Elmo Williams, then head of British production for Twentieth Century-Fox. But it was put out in the way thought likely to make the most money, and when it didn't make the money warranted in terms of its budget, that was that.

Of course this was silly; but 99 per cent of the people who are handling films in the Western world handle films just this way. If a film has strength, as they say, it shows right away, if it hasn't, down the drain. The idea that a film might not show its strength for two or three years, or only through being gradually let out while audiences are prepared, somehow doesn't apply to the vast majority of the big distributors. The thing which does apply to them—and it is something which has always baffled me—is that they devote their lives to selling a product which essentially they don't like. Many marketers of films don't go to films, they don't know about films, and they don't like films, excepting at the lowest common denominator which they not only cater to but largely help to make.

When these people come to see a film which you and a lot of other people have killed yourselves over for six months or a year, they look at this piece of your life while talking to a minor executive, or dictating to a secretary, or taking phone calls, even going out of the projection room for ten minutes at a time, or leaving after three or four reels. I dare say there are plenty of films I don't want to see all the way through, and which don't deserve concentrated attention; but I have the arrogance to presume mine do, and so I suppose does everybody else who makes films. But it isn't a question of *my* films; this is a pattern of these executives, and it is peculiar to the film industry. Of course, in America at least, films began, literally, in the hands of whorehouse operators, and their object, obviously, wasn't to appreciate the product of their clients.

6: Collaborators

Unlike some directors who either give up on a bad script or else send it up, one senses that you always try to play fair; but in some of those early British films, one also senses a kind of irony behind their worst excesses. Is this so?

There was, but it was a desperate irony because I was so badly in need of work and under such extreme pressure. This can be dangerous, because Tennessee Williams, for instance, had been told by all sorts of people who are not qualified to comment—people with whom I've never worked and who therefore don't know how I work—that I'm death on writers, that I cut ruthlessly, that I have no respect for a script. This couldn't be more untrue. Of course if I get a script which is a piece of nonsense, I will say I'll do it only if it is rewritten; of course if I get a script even from a writer I've previously worked with successfully, and the script isn't right, I will start all over again with another script. But once there *is* a script, one I believe I can do and is right, I never make any change without consulting the writer. And when I say consulting, if he's available, he makes the change himself. I don't make cuts or even line changes, and this can be testified to by the two writers I have worked with most, Evan Jones and Pinter. The only line changed in *Accident* was changed by Pinter's wife, Vivien Merchant, with his consent and my approval—a very slight change. I *believe* in the writer's contribution and I foster it. It annoys me, these judgments

passed by people who are presumably colleagues and who have no basis for making them: it's like all the people who said to me Charles Laughton is impossibly difficult, Wilfrid Lawson is hopelessly irresponsible; absolutely untrue in both cases, though maybe true in other circumstances. Like the man who said to me last night, "I've dealt with people who are terribly difficult, almost as difficult as you"—and he'd met me fifteen minutes before, didn't know a damn thing about whether I'm difficult or not. I'm not difficult. I'm obstinate; I'm insistent on quality; and I fight like hell for it. And of course this is very inconvenient for some people.

How do you like to work with writers?

There's no rule, any more than there is any rule about how I work with actors. It depends on the subject, it depends on the writer, and it probably depends on my particular mood. Unfortunately I've had more often than not to start with subjects adapted from books or plays not of my own choice, or sometimes bad screenplays written on commission, simply because the majority of distributors, as sources of money, feel more secure with a property which has been, as they say, 'established', even if it hasn't been successful. I have tried, particularly in Europe, to work with writers who are not necessarily film writers. Evan Jones, for instance, had never written a film when he first worked with me; I had read a good bit of his work, and I'd seen two of his plays on television. In this particular case I was teaching him what I knew about films—indoctrinating him, if you like—and he was learning from direct experience. The first thing he did for me was something he had to come in on at the last moment, and he worked all the way through the shooting; so it isn't fair to judge his first performance, *The Damned*, as you would a script by someone who'd had several months to work on his own. Since then he's done four screenplays with me, and we've worked very closely on all of them. He works very fast, we talk at length, I tell him the things I don't want and the things I do, we sometimes argue, he goes off and writes, and when he's got enough he wants to show

On location for *Eve*: Losey and Jeanne Moreau

me, or a problem, he calls me up and we go on from there. In the process of shooting we may find things we want to develop out of locations or out of the peculiarities of a certain actor.

Prior to that, take *Blind Date*, which as I've said was something that came of pressures, including the blacklist. I knew both Ben Barzman and Millard Lampell, having worked with Ben twice before, with Millard not at all, though we'd known each other for many years. It was a question of getting a script in four weeks or not at all. We decided that Millard Lampell was better able to write the romantic scenes, and Ben the rest. So they divided the sequences that way, and then I put them together; sometimes they crossed over, and Millard would re-write something of Ben's, Ben something of Millard's.

In the case of *The Criminal*, I was given a script which I considered absolute nonsense, with even a bad structure, but which contained certain melodramatic elements the producers wanted to back. I got in Alun Owen, who had not been writing very long and not at all for films, and whose gift at that time was largely auditory: he could reproduce dialect and speech rhythms, and he was an extraordinary observer of character. With him, I had regular morning sessions. He would work all night, and before I went to the studio in the morning I would stop by and listen to what he'd done, which more often than not was tape-recorded. He gave *The Criminal* a kind of authenticity, and an immediacy and interest it wouldn't otherwise have had.

With Pinter, we had various discussions over a period of years, and when we finally came to work on *The Servant*, he'd already written a screenplay which I thought was 75 per cent bad and unproduceable, but had a number of scenes which were not changed as they reached the screen. I gave him a very long list of rewrites which enraged him, and we had an almost disastrous first session. He said he was not accustomed to being worked with this way—neither was I, for that matter—but he came to see me the next day, I tore up the notes, and we started through the script. Since then we've never had any difficulty at all. With Harold now, it's a question of detailed discussion of intent; then he usually

Shooting *Accident*: Bogarde, Alexander Knox, Stanley Baker, Pinter, Losey

writes a first draft, which I comment on, and which he then rewrites; and there may or may not be small rewrites during the course of shooting—more often than not there aren't. I may ask for additions, there may be tiny things within a scene—he's very often around during shooting, as is Evan Jones.

With Hugo Butler, who was much my superior and senior in experience, and who did the major part of the writing on *The Prowler*, we worked very closely, discussing everything. But I felt like a pupil to his teacher because I was still overawed by Hollywood and he was an extremely skilled screenwriter. But when he came to writing *Eve* . . . a long time had passed between those two pictures, although I had done some very pleasant work with him in between on *The Big Night*. He was blacklisted almost as soon as we began work on *The Big Night*, and in order to finish it, he went off to a cabin in the mountains with me where we worked all day every

The two textures in *Blind Date*

day on the script, just the two of us, without a secretary, cooking our own food, so we wouldn't be interrupted by the constabulary until it was finished. When it came to *Eve*, Hugo was very good as always on structure, and very good on many other things, but basically he didn't agree with me about the subject of the film. He had quite a different idea about the relationship of men and

women, so finally we couldn't agree and I brought Evan Jones in
on it. This was a much more active collaboration, I would say, than
any other I've had; and I probably made a greater personal
contribution to that script than any of the others.

On *Modesty Blaise*, there were four or five early scripts, the first
of which I never read. The first one I did read was Sidney

Gilliat's, and it had many of the elements which are in the film; I liked it, and it was what made me accept, though I thought it needed a lot of work. I was then confronted with a script by Suso Cecchi D'Amico, for which a vast sum of money had been paid and which wasn't any use for my purposes. So that was dismissed, and Evan and I went to work, using the Sidney Gilliat script as a basis, but also using new locations, new ideas about actors and approaches, and so on. The writing went on right from the beginning of the picture to the end, and even afterwards to some extent, in the added narration and an occasional additional or changed line.

On Blind Date, *was your use of two writers purely a practical arrangement? There is a noticeable difference in texture, both visually and in the writing, between the love scenes and the rest of the film; and you have said you wanted the love scenes all to be daytime. How much was this designed?*

The idea of placing the love scenes during the day was certainly designed, for the usual mixed reasons, which may not be entirely good ones. In the first place because it is always assumed, particularly in films, that people make love physically only in the dark, which is of course absolute nonsense; and secondly because in terms of the characters' relationship, it was the only time they could. But the texture *is* different, and it is a question of there being two different writers, two *very* different writers. I think the division made between them was right, but it was made primarily because the script had to be delivered within four weeks. We had to shoot then or not make the picture at all. I had been given a script I simply couldn't shoot—I just didn't know how to begin, and I don't think it would have worked. So it was a practical necessity because of the usual kinds of stupidity, because I had been nearly two years without work, and because neither of the scriptwriters, although both were and are important writers, had had a credit on a film or anything else for very close to ten years. And since one of the conditions was that they were to have a credit, it was equally important to them.

The Criminal

You were unhappy with the original script of The Criminal*: to what extent are you happy with the film as completed?*

To say I was unhappy with the original is an understatement: it was an unbelievably phony, vulgar, cheap script containing certain melodramatic elements which—in my opinion anyway—were largely taken out of old American prison films, and which had little or nothing to do with English society. At no time was I even vaguely interested in that script, but it was offered to me and to Stanley Baker. Having worked together on *Blind Date*, we each said we'd do it if the other agreed; and in that combination there was a certain degree of strength, although not as much as you might think, which made it possible for me to get an entirely fresh script.

But, as always, there were insistences on the part of the producers that certain specific melodramatic or sensational elements they thought were commercial had to be kept. Mostly the exterior, out-of-the-prison scenes: the love affairs, the informing, and the race-track robbery. I must say the distributors were bitterly disappointed in my robbery, because they wanted me to do a *Rififi* and I didn't see any reason to, nor did I wish to compete—a robbery is a robbery unless you can do it as well as Dassin did. It seemed to me the important thing was to see the exterior aspect, see the men assembling for the robbery, know what they were doing, see where they were going, see how they got in, and then see them come out and escape. The fact that inside somebody points a gun at somebody else, and someone puts lots of money into satchels, is not to me very interesting. The distributors, I think, still regret it; and this kind of thing occasionally means my films aren't handled as well as they might be, because they say, "Oh well, he made *his* film, he didn't make *ours*." Well, I make my film, and I don't know what their film is.

Looking through your credits, and considering the fact that your films are noted for having a 'Losey style', it is surprising that you have so seldom worked with the same cameraman twice.

This isn't a matter of choice. I prefer to work with people I have already worked with successfully. For example, I loved working with Roy Hunt on *The Dividing Line*. He, quite unfairly, was not considered a top Hollywood cameraman, and so when I came to *The Prowler* he was unacceptable. Instead, I was given Arthur Miller—with whom I worked with the greatest of pleasure. I tried to get him again but he became ill; he was a strange little man who'd been a jockey, suffered several accidents, and had tuberculosis, and he was simply physically unable. I also liked very much working with Ernest Laszlo on *M* but couldn't get him for *The Big Night*, something which often happens because you can't make a commitment ahead the way I was working.

In this country . . . let's skip up to *Blind Date*. I loved working with Chris Challis, and have tried to get him on practically every film since, but he is so popular both personally and professionally that he was never available when I wanted him. In the case of Gianni Di Venanzo, he was a most disagreeable and difficult man whom I learned to love, and whose work and manner of work I admired enormously—excepting for his violent tempers and abuse of his subordinates, which may perhaps have just been an Italian characteristic, exaggerated by me. I can think of no other cameraman in whom I had so much pleasure as far as result was concerned, or, strangely enough, so much rapport with despite the language difficulties.

The man who did *The Damned*, Arthur Grant, is I think far superior to any opportunities he has been given, and I would gladly have worked with him again, but there were many obstacles, not the least of them being that he was under contract to Hammer; being a man well into years, he had to have security, which I couldn't offer. I adored working with Douglas Slocombe and Chic Waterson as operator on *The Servant*, and not only tried to get them, but gave them first opportunity on every picture I've made since then. Each wanted to work with me, but also wanted the security offered them by a term contract from Fox. On *King and Country* I did have Chic Waterson, which was a great boon, and a cameraman with whom I disagreed most of the time.

So far as *Accident* is concerned, I couldn't get Douglas Slocombe, who was my first choice; even if Di Venanzo were allowed to work in this country, he was dead; I couldn't get Chris Challis. Gerry Fisher had been the operator on *Modesty Blaise*, and I liked the way he worked. I gave him three days to decide whether he wanted to try as a lighting cameraman, whether he could, and told him if he said he could, I would accept him. In somewhat less than three days he said he could, and did, and he's done a brilliant job. There are foreign cameramen I'd like to work with, too: Henri Decaë who did the Venice Festival footage on *Eve*, for instance, and Sacha Vierny, who has done a lot of work with Resnais.

The main problem is that if you're working independently and can't provide security for people who don't get enough money to live between films, you can't ask them to wait for something nebulous; so the chances of their being available when you want them are very slight. I think Douglas Slocombe and to some extent even Chris Challis, and certainly Gerry Fisher, have a kind of prior loyalty to me; but I can't avail myself of it if I can't give them assurances. The continuity you spoke of comes partly from the fact that I had Richard MacDonald on all my European films except *Accident*, but also because I think I have been fairly consistent, and because I am fairly articulate and definite about what I want from everybody, but particularly where sets and camera are concerned . . . although knowing nothing technically, I must say.

In your attitude to actors, you obviously don't share Bresson's mistrust—what Godard has called his racism towards professional actors. Nor do you seem to feel like Godard, who, with one or two exceptions like Karina and Belmondo, prefers—especially in small parts—to use actors only once, perhaps seeing something he can use and then having no further use for it. You have what one might almost call a repertory company à la John Ford, with actors like Alexander Knox and James Villiers whom you use almost as symbols. . . . Put it this way: why did you cast Alexander Knox in Accident *when you might have used any one of a dozen character actors?*

It's not quite as simple as that. For one thing, a lot of these actors are willing to work for me now in small parts, which they wouldn't do for somebody else; and I'm not so sure I could get someone else as good. That's one thing, and that's part of building up a company . . . it's not a company because one can't sustain it, but it's the *wish*. The other thing is, I think you will find I also use people for what I can get out of one particular appearance, as you say Godard does. Take, for example, the girl in the orgy in *The Servant* who sits in front of the picture: I've never used her before or since. That was it, that was the particular thing I wanted . . . and I could give you other instances.

The attitude Godard describes as racist on the part of Bresson I think applies equally to Antonioni, and to a number of other directors, and it's one I don't hold with at all. I feel that you terribly restrict your own film if you don't allow everyone to use himself to his utmost capacity at that particular moment. This is another reason for repeating with actors. There are all sorts of other reasons which have to do with attitudes, with progression as an actor, with explorations of the actor's particular vulnerabilities and potentials; but these aren't possible unless you have worked together before and unless you have a language, unless you trust each other . . . you trust what the actor can do, and the actor trusts you not to let him make a fool of himself.

Perhaps the most striking tribute to your attitude and methods is the way someone like Dirk Bogarde has developed into a remarkable actor virtually through your films.

Dirk Bogarde has had a curious professional life in that he has been, in English terms at least, a very big popular star, and is now recognised internationally as an extraordinary actor. I don't think these things are invented, they come about through various kinds of growth; and I certainly can't claim responsibility for his growth; it was intrinsic in him. But when I came to this country and did my first picture anonymously, *The Sleeping Tiger*, it was condemned to the B category by virtue of its script and budget—and I have never been very happy about B categories, even when they were pretty well pressed upon me. I had been told about Bogarde, whom I had never seen; and after I had been told he'd turned it down and it was quite impossible because of his salary and because he wouldn't consider working under these conditions, I went through with a screening which had already been set up of a film called *Hunted*. I found him so good and sensitive, I immediately said I didn't care whether he'd turned it down or not, or what his price was, I wanted to see him. So we had lunch at his house, and I persuaded him to come and see *The Prowler*. Immediately after that, he said yes. Without that my life might have been very different; it didn't immediately affect his, excepting possibly adversely, as *The Sleeping Tiger* didn't do very well.

Then we remained friends but didn't see each other very often.

Five varieties of Bogarde: *The Sleeping Tiger, The Servant, King and Country, Modesty Blaise, Accident*

We tried to get together on a Rank situation four or five years later, which ended in disaster for both of us, not through the fault of either . . . and we still had a desire to work together. Then came *The Servant*, very nearly ten years after *The Sleeping Tiger*, and in between I had not seen one single picture Dirk had made—I have told him this, so it's no violation of anything. All I had seen of his was *Hunted*, *The Sleeping Tiger*, and a play he did with Peter Hall. So I decided I'd better see what he'd been doing in between, and saw *Victim*, which I respected but didn't like, neither the performance nor the picture; I looked at a bit of *The Password is Courage* and walked out; and that's all. Since then we have worked together in many different ways and on many different things, and the only additional film of his I've seen is *Darling*, in which I think he's brilliant. So I didn't base myself at all on what I'd seen, I based myself on him, and he, I think, has based himself on me. We have been mutually helpful. I don't know whether Dirk has seen pictures I've made without him—he probably hasn't, and no reason particularly why he should. We've developed separately towards the same end, I guess.

How much do you collaborate with your actors? From your films it looks obvious that you don't work in the same way as, say, Antonioni, whose actors, one gathers, have no idea what is going on.

This is a very difficult question, because I don't really know the answer. Dirk has said publicly on many occasions, and he's said it to me too, that I don't tell him anything but that he always knows. I think this is true and untrue: I do tell him more than he thinks. But in any event I talk to actors as I think they want to be talked to. Some want to be talked to in highly subjective terms, others don't and can't use it; and the same thing is true of the various methods which may be brought to bear on a particular scene. The main thing is getting a responsive relationship between the director and the actor, and a protective one. A protective relationship, I think, is essential for everyone working on a film; and the major responsibility for the protective, or if you like father role is the director's; but he also has to be lover. Without that, nothing happens in my opinion. Antonioni would disagree heartily—I think he regards all actors as enemies. But what any particular actor wants at any particular time may be quite different, and you can't always supply the need; sometimes, if there is communication, a few words can result in a whole new vista for both.

A piece of casting which caused a lot of raised eyebrows—before the event, not after—was Stanley Baker in Accident. *Can you say why you chose him for that part?*

For the same reasons I've already given: the extension of areas of work and the ways of working develop each time you work with an actor who is responsive and wants to develop, to extend himself. And for all of the other things which may not relate directly to the performance: an actor's willingness to subjugate himself to the film rather than play at starring and be competitive . . . for reasons of loyalty, for reasons of sacrifice, all sorts of things. Also I thought the combination of Dirk and Stanley was a very good one, and it was one which was ultimately financeable, although with great difficulty. Also because I knew from several pictures, in each of which the performances are quite different, that he could do it. I always go with actors on feel, not on what they have done. And I never ask for auditions; almost never for screen tests—only if I am dubious about how someone will photograph.

The thing all of us desire is security and continuity, but it's one of the frightful contradictions of the whole economic structure of the film industry that you have this vast investment, this vast speculation, and the failures have to be paid for. I was talking to a distributor recently, who said, "You complain about distribution charges being 33⅓ per cent on your pictures, and ask how distribution can cost so much; and my answer is, it doesn't. But we have to pay for the pictures that fail. In a major company, if we get one out of eight that hits, we're lucky." I'm sure this is true. It's bitter that one has to pay for other people's failures . . . but all these things are part of the reality of making films, unless you make them on a

Stanley Baker with Sam Wanamaker in *The Criminal*, with Jeanne Moreau in *Eve*

shoestring or outside the union orbit, which is neither interesting nor very good beyond a certain point. But if you are going to face that reality, then it's very hard indeed to keep a company of actors, equally hard to keep a company of technicians. I can't. I've never made vast sums of money, I never have any margin between one picture and the next, I always have to wait (I mean I always insist on waiting, but this amounts to having to wait), which becomes increasingly difficult with increasing years and increasing responsibilities—increasing years not in the sense that they are weighing me down, but because I am aware of the passage of time and how much there is left to do what I want to do, and how much is consumed in the wrong things.

I can't ask a co-producer like Norman Priggen, who has been invaluable to me, or someone like Richard MacDonald to wait. I can ask myself to wait . . . but I am more spendthrift, not about personal extravagances, spendthrift of my life. Each person can exact this of himself, but he can't ask it of someone else. And up to now I have been unable to provide either continuing salaries or continuity of work to any of the people concerned; so they must make their own choices as to whether they will wait or not, whether they can afford to, whether they can take the risk, because I never know whether a picture is going to happen until the day before it does. How enviable the Russians, the Czechs, the people who work under a system of continuity . . . it may have its disadvantages, but the advantage of continuity is enormous. How enviable Godard, who can go from one picture to the next, or even do two at once. Or Bergman, who can combine theatre and films, and keep his company, his technicians, and also work in a situation where he only has the crew he needs, where the lighting cameraman may also be the operator, the prop man also the electrician, and where everybody participates in every aspect of the film. This is in no way to be construed as an attack on the unions here, or unions in general, but when you know the history of British films and American films, you understand why trade-union protections can often become syndicalist suffocations.

7: Galileo

One of your long-standing dream projects has been to film Brecht's Galileo: *how do you conceive it in film terms? Or is it too difficult a question?*

Brecht, of course, is a difficult question, and *Galileo* is even more difficult; but at the same time they're easy, because my life has been so full of *Galileo* since before I ever shot a feature film. It's all there to be stated, and usually doesn't get stated because it's such a large subject and the whole fashionableness of Brecht is an irritation—to me anyway, in the sense of all the years of struggle which produced absolutely nothing and all the people who cash in now. *Galileo* is now more or less recognised as a great play; most people forget there was a time when people thought it unreadable and amateur-ish. Even before the notorious *Variety* review of my production, Mike Todd had bought it because Orson Welles wanted to direct and Laughton to play in it; but he didn't know what it was about and didn't like it. Ultimately it was produced only because a very rich and philanthropic young friend of mine, T. Edward Hamble-ton, who has since run a repertory theatre in New York with the help of ANTA, came in for half the production costs; and because Laughton, Brecht and I, and many others, worked for nothing.

Then when *Galileo* went to New York with ANTA, the same was true; there were no salaries. I never got a penny out of *Galileo*, neither did Laughton; and in New York we finally made it a controversial commercial success. It was originally supposed to run two weeks, which was extended to three. Brooks Atkinson, then critic of the *New York Times*, wrote about it several times, attacking it; and John Mason Brown, of the *New York Post*, did the same thing but praising it. And audiences poured in. There were always fifty to a hundred standing for every performance. The run was extended for a week, but after that it was impossible because of quite legitimate commitments. Laughton and I wanted to go on into a commercial theatre, and in those days it would only have cost about $75,000 to transfer from a non-profit set-up in which no salaries were paid except to people who had to have them (in which case they got a minimum). We were prepared to do it, but the only theatre we could find couldn't guarantee us more than three weeks; and obviously nobody would put up $75,000 if they were guaranteed a run of no more than three weeks. So there it died. When I came to England, I tried to get Binkie Beaumont and countless other people to do *Galileo*, or *The Good Woman*, or *Herr Puntila*, and many others, but particularly *Galileo*, which I had spent more than a year of my life on, and which existed in an almost perfect English version written in English by Brecht with Laughton and myself present and contributing. I couldn't get a breath of interest from anybody. Then came the Berliner Ensemble as a kind of legend, then came Tynan, and since then there has been an outcrop of Brecht in what are, in my opinion, totally inferior, over-intellectualised, misunderstood productions—with the exception of the Berliner Ensemble, the Piccolo Teatro di Milano, and possibly the Théâtre National Populaire, although that too is something of a distortion. All the productions here at the Mermaid, Royal Court and the rest were ludicrous; and most of what was said about Brecht was ludicrous; and Brecht himself would have abhorred and disavowed all the influence and idolatry.

Anyway, Brecht gave me the exclusive rights to do *Galileo* in English for many years—and I couldn't get anybody to do it. It has always seemed to me that Brecht is very close to film, and that my theatre work was approaching film. However, I don't think Brecht has ever been successfully transposed into film: just as Brecht is a particular theatre idiom, which has to be understood and fully realised, likewise that same idiom in films is not capable of exact reproduction, otherwise you simply get—to make a bad comparison —Olivier's *Othello* done for Pay Television. Because of the enormous impact of the words and the content of the play, and because of its simplicity and the possibilities for realistic yet highly stylised selection of background, I had always wished to shoot in the real situations, which mostly still exist in Padua, Florence and Rome; but by means of lighting and so on, to abstract the particular things I wanted to have as backgrounds. And to keep the costumes not accurate, not literal, just as they were in the Hollywood and New York stage productions. The Prince, for instance, was dressed in a costume copied from a Renaissance portrait of a tailor; many of the other costumes were Breughel, particularly in the Carnival scene; and there was never any discrepancy because there was an overall style. Both the Hollywood and New York productions used a simple wood structure, almost a constructivist set, with the usual white curtain of Brecht (which I'm not sure was a great advantage) and slides. But always a sense of texture, and a careful selection of props. All this, I thought, could have been done in colour on the real locations.

This is where the cameraman would be so terribly important. I think with two or three of the men I have worked with, but certainly with Di Venanzo, who was the man I had in mind at the time, it would have worked; one can *select* what one wants to see, and more in colour than otherwise, even though colour is more revealing. I would make no capital at all of the fact that it was a real location; I consider the play virtually a scenario for a film, most of the scenes with the exception of the Carnival are interior, and there is no reason why with selective lighting one couldn't just see one piece of ornamentation, one fragment of décor, instead of a whole palace or a vast room which would distract the eye. The only reason for making it on location rather than in a studio, is that in a studio it is virtually impossible to get the kind of texture needed. Even an art director like Richard MacDonald, who is more likely to bring it off than anybody else in the world, even if he got

Charles Laughton as Galileo

on the set and painted it himself (which is a violation of ACTT regulations), couldn't *alone* do it. But that's what would have to be done, because if there isn't texture, there isn't anything, and there mustn't at any time be a cluttered or realistic background.

But *Galileo* was absolutely barred in Italy by the Church. Then, while I was in Italy shooting *Eve*, the Church agreed to a stage production in Milan, which opened the whole thing up. Also, by the way, the pressure of the Roman Catholic Church had barred any possibility of a film in Hollywood, because Laughton and I had tried to do it there before I left. Even though things had opened up in Italy, I still saw no way to do it until Anthony Quinn rang me to say he had a million dollars for it, could I get another million. I said I thought I could. At this point I got in touch with Stefan Brecht, and he said yes: there were two daughters, a son and Helle, who were joint executors, and this matter was theoretically under the jurisdiction of Stefan. We were proceeding when suddenly there was a veto from Helene Weigel in Berlin, which dismayed me.

I found the money, and went to Berlin for the first time since the war—to East Berlin, which took the better part of a day—and saw my old friend Helle, who had worked completely in the background in Hollywood, and who had gone to Switzerland shortly after Brecht did, before the New York production. She was exactly as I remembered her, and I asked why the objection now. She said that Barbara, who had been a fifteen-year-old high-school girl when I knew her in Hollywood, objected because she thought Quinn was not right for the part. I answered that many things could be said for or against him in this part, but it was late because they had agreed, we had gone ahead, and he was providing the money.

Helle invited me to lunch to talk about it. It was a fascinating day in which I saw the Brecht archives, and the room in which he died, where a few hours before he had said to her, "Well, at least you won't have any trouble, you can just put me out of the window down a chute"—there was a cemetery next to their house. Finally we got down to it, and Helle said—this may give you some idea of this quite extraordinary woman—"I don't know Quinn. You tell me you can do it and he's right. I want you to answer a few questions. Do you think he's the ideal person to play Galileo?" I said, "No, I don't know any ideal person; I don't think Laughton was ideal." "Do you think he will give a brilliant performance?" she asked. I said, "I think so, but I've never worked with him and I can't guarantee it." Finally she said, "When you come to me and tell me you have somebody you think is an ideal piece of casting, somebody you are sure will give a brilliant performance, I will say yes on your word. But until you tell me that, I don't think, in the light of the objections from Barbara, I should." I argued that none of us was getting younger, it was a very important play, and even if it were done imperfectly, the play was more important than the performance. When I said I couldn't guarantee a brilliant performance, I wasn't at all sure there mightn't be one; I thought there might be, I just couldn't guarantee it. I also said the money might disappear as quickly as it had come, and might not happen again in my lifetime or hers.

She said, "I'm in no hurry." And that has been the end of *Galileo*, because I cannot tell her who will give a brilliant performance. So it's impossible.

Filmography

Joseph Losey

Born La Crosse, Wisconsin, 14 January 1909

1925–29 Studied medicine at Dartmouth College; theatre activity with the Dartmouth Players

1929–30 Studied literature at the Harvard Graduate School of Arts and Sciences

1930 Began writing, mainly on theatre, for *Theatre Arts Magazine, New York Times, New York Herald Tribune, Saturday Review*; assistant stage manager with *Grand Hotel* (National Theatre, New York, 13 November)

1931 Travelled in Germany and England; stage manager with *Payment Deferred* (St. James's Theatre, London, 4 May, and Lyceum Theatre, New York, 30 September)

1932 Stage manager with *Fatal Alibi* (Booth Theatre, New York, 8 February); stage director of first two variety shows at Radio City Music Hall

1933 First stage production, *Little Ol' Boy*

1935 Travelled in Russia, Sweden, Finland; reporter for *Variety*

1938 Supervised production of sixty educational montage films for the Rockefeller Foundation's Human Relations Commission

1939 Directed first short film, *Pete Roleum and His Cousins*

1942 Worked in radio

1943 In Army Signal Corps, made two shorts for United States Production Army Pictorial

1948 Directed first feature, *The Boy With Green Hair*

1958 Began directing a series of commercials for Commercial Television

Features

The Boy with Green Hair (1948)

Production Company	R.K.O.-Radio
Executive Producer	Dore Schary
Producer	Adrian Scott, replaced by Stephen Ames
Production Manager	Ruby Rosenberg
Director	Joseph Losey
Assistant Director	James Lane
Script	Ben Barzman, Alfred Lewis Levitt. Based on a story by Betsy Beaton
Script Supervisor	Richard Kinon
Director of Photography	George Barnes
Colour Process	Technicolor
Colour Consultants	Natalie Kalmus, Morgan Padelford
Camera Operator	Eddie Pyle
Editor	Frank Doyle
Design Consultant	John Hubley
Art Directors	Albert S. D'Agostino, Ralph Berger
Set Decorators	Darrell Silvera, William Stevens
Music	Leigh Harline
Musical Director	Constantin Bakaleinikoff
Song "Nature Boy"	Eden Ahbez
Costumes	Adele Balkan
Sound	Earl Wolcott, Clem Portman

Dean Stockwell (*Peter Frye*), Pat O'Brien (*Gramp*), Robert Ryan (*Dr. Evans*), Barbara Hale (*Miss Brand*), Samuel S. Hinds (*Dr. Knudson*), Walter Catlett (*The King*), Richard Lyon (*Michael*), Charles Meredith (*Mr. Piper*), Regis Toomey (*Mr. Davis*), David Clarke (*The Barber*), Billy Sheffield (*Red*), John Calkins (*Danny*), Teddy Infuhr (*Timmy*), Dwayne Hickman (*Joey*), Eilene Janssen (*Peggy*), Charles Arnt (*Mr. Hammond*), Russ Tamblyn and Curtis Jackson (*Pupils*).

Filmed at R.K.O. Studios in 36 days. First shown at a Hollywood preview, 19 November 1948; U.S. release, 8 January 1949; G.B., 26 June 1950. Running time, 82 mins.
Distributors: R.K.O.-Radio (U.S./G.B.)

The Lawless (1949)

Production Company	Paramount. A Pine-Thomas Production
Producers	William H. Pine, William C. Thomas
Director	Joseph Losey

Script	Geoffrey Homes [i.e. Daniel Mainwaring]. Based on his own novel, *The Voice of Stephen Wilder*
Director of Photography	Roy Hunt
Editor	Howard Smith
Design Consultant	John Hubley
Art Director	Lewis H. Creber
Set Decorator	Al Kegerris
Music	Mahlon Merrick
Musical Director	David Chudnow

Macdonald Carey (*Larry Wilder*), Gail Russell (*Sunny Garcia*), Lalo Rios (*Paul Rodriguez*), John Sands (*Joe Ferguson*), Lee Patrick (*Jan Dawson*), John Hoyt (*Ed Ferguson*), Maurice Jara (*Lopo Chavez*), Walter Reed (*Jim Wilson*), Guy Anderson (*Jonas Creel*), Argentina Brunetti (*Mrs. Rodriguez*), William Edmunds (*Mr. Jensen*), Gloria Winters (*Mildred Jensen*), John Davis (*Harry Pawling*), Martha Hyer (*Caroline Tyler*), Frank Fenton (*Mr. Prentiss*), Paul Harvey (*Blake, the Chief of Police*), Ian MacDonald (*Sergeant Al Peters*), Robert B. Williams (*Boswell*), Julia Faye (*Mrs. Jensen*), Pedro De Cordoba (*Mr. Garcia*), Frank Ferguson (*Carl Green*), John Murphy (*Mayor*), Tab Hunter, Felipe Turich, Noel Reyburn, Russ Conway, James Bush, Howard Negley, Gordon Nelson, Ray Hyke.

Filmed on location at Marysville and Grass Valley, California, in 23 days. First shown in London, 4 May 1950; U.S.A., July 1950. Running time, 83 mins.
Distributors: Paramount (U.S./G.B.)
G.B. title: *The Dividing Line*

The Prowler (1951)

Production Company	Horizon Pictures
Producer	S. P. Eagle [i.e. Sam Spiegel]
Associate Producer	Samuel Rheiner
Production Manager	Joseph H. Nadel
Director	Joseph Losey
Assistant Director	Robert Aldrich
Script	Dalton Trumbo, Hugo Butler. From an original story by Robert Thoeren, Hans Wilhelm
Script Supervisor	Don Weis
Director of Photography	Arthur Miller
Editor	Paul Weatherwax

Design Consultant	John Hubley
Art Director	Boris Leven
Set Decorator	Jacques Mapes
Music	Lyn Murray
Musical Director	Irving Friedman
Song "Baby"	Lyn Murray, Dick Mack
Song sung by	Bob Carroll
Costumes	Maria Donovan
Sound	Benny Winkler

Van Heflin (*Webb Garwood*), Evelyn Keyes (*Susan Gilvray*), John Maxwell (*Bud Crocker*), Katherine Warren (*Mrs. Crocker*), Emerson Treacy (*William Gilvray*), Madge Blake (*Martha Gilvray*), Wheaton Chambers (*Dr. James*), Robert Osterloh (*Coroner*), Sherry Hall (*John Gilvray*), Louise Lorimer (*Motel Manager*), George Nader (*Photographer*), Benny Burt (*Journalist*), Tiny Jones.

Filmed in studio and on location in the Californian desert in 17 days. First shown in U.S.A., 25 May 1951; G.B., 2 November 1951. Running time, 92 mins.
Distributors: United Artists (U.S./G.B.)

M (1951)

Production Company	Columbia
Producer	Seymour Nebenzal
Associate Producer	Harold Nebenzal
Production Manager	Ben Hersh
Director	Joseph Losey
Assistant Director	Robert Aldrich
Script	Norman Reilly Raine, Leo Katcher. Based on the original script by Thea von Harbou and Fritz Lang
Additional Dialogue	Waldo Salt
Script Supervisor	Don Weis
Director of Photography	Ernest Laszlo
Editor	Edward Mann
Design Consultant	John Hubley
Art Director	Martin Obzina
Set Decorator	Ray Robinson
Music	Michel Michelet
Musical Director	Bert Shefter
Sound	Leon Becker, Mac Dalgleish

David Wayne (*Martin Harrow*), Howard Da Silva (*Carney*), Luther Adler (*Langley*), Martin Gabel (*Marshall*), Steve Brodie (*Lieut. Becker*), Raymond Burr (*Pottsy*), Glenn Anders (*Riggert*), Karen Morley (*Mrs. Coster*), Norman Lloyd (*Sutro*), John Miljan (*Blind Vendor*), Walter Burke (*MacMahan*), Roy Engel (*Regan*), Benny Burt (*Jansen*), Lennie Bremen (*Lemke*), Jim Backus (*The Mayor*), Janine Perreau (*Intended Victim*), Robin Fletcher (*Elsie Coster*), Bernard Szold (*Nightwatchman*), Jorja Curtright (*Mrs. Stewart*).

Filmed on location in Los Angeles and at Columbia Studios in 20 days. First shown in U.S.A., March 1951; G.B., 21 December 1951. Running time, 88 mins. (82 mins. in G.B.)
Distributors: Columbia (U.S./G.B.)

The Big Night (1951)

Production Company	Philip Waxman
Producer	Philip A. Waxman
Director	Joseph Losey
Assistant Director	Ivan Volkman
Script	Hugo Butler, Ring Lardner Jnr., Stanley Ellin, Joseph Losey. Based on the novel *Dreadful Summit* by Stanley Ellin
Script Supervisor	Arnold Laven
Director of Photography	Hal Mohr
Editor	Edward Mann
Art Director	Nicholas Remisoff
Special Effects	Ray Mercer, Lee Zavitz
Music	Lyn Murray
Musical Director	Leon Klatzkin
Song	Lyn Murray, Sid Kuller
Costumes	Joseph King
Sound	Leon Becker

John Barrymore Jnr. (*Georgie La Main*), Preston Foster (*Andy La Main*), Howland Chamberlin (*Flanagan*), Howard St. John (*Al Judge*), Dorothy Comingore (*Julie Rostina*), Joan Lorring (*Marion Rostina*), Philip Bourneuf (*Dr. Lloyd Cooper*), Emil Meyer (*Peckinpaugh*), Mauri Lynn (*Terry Angelus*), Myron Healey (*Kennealy*), Joseph Mell (*Mr. Ehrlich*), Robert Aldrich (*Spectator at boxing-match*), Joe McTurk, Pick Lamar, Patricia Enright, Teresa Enright.

Filmed in studio in 24 days. First shown in U.S.A., 7 December 1951; G.B., 1953. Running time, 75 mins. (71 mins. in G.B.) Distributors: United Artists (U.S./G.B.)

Stranger on the Prowl (1952)

Production Company	Consorzio Produttori Cinematografici Tirrenia/Riviera Film Inc.
Executive Producer	Alfonso Bajocci
Producer	Noel Calef
Director	Andrea Forzano [i.e. Joseph Losey]
Script	Andrea Forzano [i.e. Ben Barzman]. Based on a story by Noel Calef
Director of Photography	Henri Alekan
Editor	Thelma Connell
Art Director	Antonio Valente
Music	G. C. Sonzogno
Sound	Leon Becker

Paul Muni (*The Man*), Joan Lorring (*Angela*), Vittorio Manunta (*Giacomo Fontana*), Luisa Rossi (*Giacomo's Mother*), Aldo Silvani (*Peroni*), Franco Balducci (*Morelli*), Enrico Glori (*Signor Pucci*), Arnoldo Foà (*The Inspector*), Elena Manson (*The Storekeeper*), Alfredo Varelli (*Castelli*), Fausta Mazzunchelli (*Giacomo's Sister*), Cesare Trapani (*Giacomo's Friend*), Léon Lenoir (*Mancini*), Linda Sini (*Signora Raffetto*), Giulio Marchetti (*Signor Raffetto*), Noel Calef (*Flute-player*), Henri Alekan (*Priest on bicycle*), Nando Bruno, Ave Ninchi.

Filmed at Tirrenia Studios and on location at Taranto, Livorno and Pisa, in 86 days. First shown in Italy, May 1952; U.S.A., 2 November 1953; G.B., 30 April 1954. Running time, 100 mins. (82 mins. in U.S.A./G.B.) Distributors: United Artists (U.S./G.B.) Italian title: *Imbarco a Mezzanotte*; G.B. title: *Encounter*

The Sleeping Tiger (1954)

Production Company	Insignia
Producer	Victor Hanbury
Production Manager	Ted Holliday
Director	Victor Hanbury [i.e. Joseph Losey]
Assistant Director	Denis Johnson
Script	Derek Frye [i.e. Harold Buchman, Carl Foreman]. Based on the novel by Maurice Moiseiwitsch

Director of Photography	Harry Waxman
Camera Operators	James Bawden, Dudley Lovell
Editor	Reginald Mills
Design Consultant	Richard MacDonald
Art Director	John Stoll
Music	Malcolm Arnold
Musical Director	Muir Mathieson
Sound	W. H. Lindop, C. Poulton

Dirk Bogarde (*Frank Clements*), Alexis Smith (*Glenda Esmond*), Alexander Knox (*Dr. Clive Esmond*), Hugh Griffith (*Inspector Simmons*), Patricia McCarron (*Sally*), Maxine Audley (*Carol*), Glyn Houston (*Bailey*), Harry Towb (*Harry*), Russell Waters (*Manager*), Billie Whitelaw (*Receptionist*), Fred Griffiths (*Taxi-driver*), Esma Cannon (*Window-cleaner*).

Filmed at Nettlefold Studios, December 1953–January 1954. First shown in London, 24 June 1954; U.S.A., October 1954. Running time, 89 mins. Distributors: Anglo Amalgamated (G.B.), Astor (U.S.)

The Intimate Stranger (1956)

Production Company	Anglo Guild
Producer	Alec C. Snowden
Production Manager	Jim O'Connolly
Director	Joseph Walton [i.e. Joseph Losey]
Assistant Director	Bill Shore
Script	Peter Howard [i.e. Howard Koch]
Director of Photography	Gerald Gibbs
Camera Operator	Brian Rhodes
Editor	Geoffrey Muller
Design Consultant	Richard MacDonald
Art Director	Wilfred Arnold
Music	Trevor Duncan
Musical Director	Richard Taylor
Costumes	Alice McLaren
Sound	Sidney Rider, Ron Abbott

Richard Basehart (*Reggie Wilson*), Mary Murphy (*Evelyn Stewart*), Constance Cummings (*Kay Wallace*), Roger Livesey (*Ben Case*), Mervyn Johns (*Ernest Chaple*), Faith Brook (*Lesley Wilson*), Vernon Greeves (*George Mearns*), Andre Mikhelson (*Steve Vadney*), Basil Dignam (*Dr. Gray*), Grace Denbeigh-Russell (*Mrs. Lynton*), Frederick Steger (*Jenner*), Wilfred Downing (*Office Boy*), Edna Landor (*Miss Tyson*), Jack Stewart

(*Gateman*), David Lodge (*Police Sergeant Brown*), Michael Ward (*Sydney*), Jay Denyer (*Studio Policeman*), Katherine Page (*Miss Sedgwick*), Douglas Hayes (*Draper*), Lian-Shin Yang (*Mary*), Joseph Losey (*The Director*), Michael Segal (*Waiter*), Peter Verness (*Policeman*), Marianne Stone (*Martine Vadney*), Gordon Harris (*Actor*), Garfield Morgan (*Waiter*), John Preston (*Fred*), David Hurst (*Dave Pearson*), Richard Grant (*Harry*).

Filmed at Merton Park Studios, and Elstree Studios (sound-studio sequence), November–December 1955. First shown in London, 25 May 1956; U.S.A., October 1956. Running time, 95 mins. (71 mins. in U.S.A.) Distributors: Anglo Amalgamated (G.B.), R.K.O.-Radio (U.S.) U.S. title: *Finger of Guilt*

Time Without Pity (1957)

Production Company	Harlequin
Executive Producer	Leon Clore
Producers	John Arnold, Anthony Simmons
Production Manager	Leigh Aman
Director	Joseph Losey
Assistant Directors	Adrian Pryce-Jones, Colin Brewer
Script	Ben Barzman. Based on the play *Someone Waiting* by Emlyn Williams
Director of Photography	Freddie Francis
Camera Operator	Arthur Ibbetson
Editor	Alan Osbiston
Design Consultant	Richard MacDonald
Production Designer	Reece Pemberton
Art Director	Bernard Sarron
Music	Tristram Cary
Musical Director	Marcus Dods
Sound	Cyril Collick

Michael Redgrave (*David Graham*), Ann Todd (*Honor Stanford*), Leo McKern (*Robert Stanford*), Peter Cushing (*Jeremy Clayton*), Alec Mc-Cowen (*Alec Graham*), Renee Houston (*Mrs. Harker*), Paul Daneman (*Brian Stanford*), Lois Maxwell (*Vicky Harker*), Richard Wordsworth (*Maxwell*), George Devine (*Barnes*), Joan Plowright (*Agnes Cole*), Ernest Clark (*Under-Secretary*), Peter Copley (*Padre*), Hugh Moxey (*Prison Governor*), Julian Somers (*1st Warder*), John Chandos (*1st Journalist*), Dickie Henderson Jnr. (*The Comedian*), Richard Leech (*Proprietor of Espresso Bar*), Christina Lubicz (*Jenny Cole*).

Filmed at Merton Park Studios and on location in London, June–August

1956. First shown in London, 21 March 1957: U.S.A., January 1958.
Running time, 88 mins.
Distributors: Eros (G.B.), Astor (U.S.)

The Gypsy and the Gentleman (1957)

Production Company	Rank
Producer	Maurice Cowan
Director	Joseph Losey
Assistant Director	Robert Asher
Script	Janet Green. Based on the novel *Darkness I Leave You* by Nina Warner Hooke
Director of Photography	Jack Hildyard
Colour Process	Eastman Colour
Camera Operator	Jim Bawden
Editor	Reginald Beck
Design Consultant	Richard MacDonald
Art Director	Ralph Brinton
Set Decorator	Vernon Dixon
Music/Musical Director	Hans May
Costumes	Julie Harris
Sound Editor	Jim Groom
Sound Recordists	Robert T. MacPhee, Gordon K. McCallum
Historical Adviser	Vyvyan Holland

Melina Mercouri (*Belle*), Keith Michell (*Sir Paul Deverill*), Patrick McGoohan (*Jess*), June Laverick (*Sarah Deverill*), Lyndon Brook (*John Patterson*), Flora Robson (*Mrs. Haggard*), Clare Austin (*Vanessa*), Helen Haye (*Lady Ayrton*), Newton Blick (*Ruddock*), Mervyn Johns (*Brook*), John Salew (*Duffin*), Gladys Boot (*Mrs. Mortimer*), Edna Morris (*Mrs. Piggott*), Catherine Feller (*Hattie*), Laurence Naismith (*Forrester*), David Hart (*Will*), Louis Aquilina (*Coco*), Nigel Green (*The Game Pup*), Laurence Taylor (*Cropped Harry*).

Filmed at Pinewood Studios and on location at Oxhey Golf Course, June–September 1957. First shown in London, 2 February 1958; U.S.A., August 1958. Running time, 107 mins. (90 mins. in U.S.A.)
Distributors: Rank (G.B./U.S.)

Blind Date (1959)

Production Company	Independent Artists. A Julian Wintle-Leslie Parkyn Production
Producer	David Deutsch

Production Manager	George Mills
Director	Joseph Losey
Assistant Director	René Dupont
Script	Ben Barzman, Millard Lampell. Based on the novel by Leigh Howard
Director of Photography	Christopher Challis
Camera Operator	John Harris
Editor	Reginald Mills
Design Consultant	Richard MacDonald
Supervising Art Director	Edward Carrick
Art Director	Harry Pottle
Music	Richard Bennett
Musical Director	Malcolm Arnold
Costumes	Morris Angel
Sound Editor	Malcolm Cooke
Sound Recordist	Len Page
Sound Re-recordist	Ken Cameron

Hardy Krüger (*Jan Van Rooyen*), Stanley Baker (*Inspector Morgan*), Micheline Presle (*Lady Fenton, called Jacqueline Cousteau*), Robert Flemyng (*Sir Brian Lewis*), Gordon Jackson (*Police Sergeant*), John Van Eyssen (*Inspector Westover*), Jack MacGowran (*Postman*), George Roubicek (*Police Constable*), Redmond Phillips (*Police Doctor*), Lee Montague (*Sergeant Farrow*), Shirley Davien (*Girl on bus*), Christina Lubicz (*The real Jacqueline Cousteau*).

Filmed at Beaconsfield Studios and on location in London, March–April 1959. First shown in London, 20 August 1959; U.S.A., March 1960. Running time, 95 mins.
Distributors: Rank (G.B.), Paramount (U.S.)
U.S. title: *Chance Meeting*

The Criminal (1960)

Production Company	Merton Park Studios
Producer	Jack Greenwood
Associate Producer	J. P. O'Connolly
Production Manager	Bill Shore
Director	Joseph Losey
Assistant Director	Buddy Booth
Script	Alun Owen. Based on an original story by Jimmy Sangster

Director of Photography	Robert Krasker
Camera Operator	John Harris
Editor	Reginald Mills
Design Consultant	Richard MacDonald
Art Director	Scott Macgregor
Music/Musical Director	Johnny Dankworth
Song "Prison Blues"	sung by Cleo Laine
Sound	Sidney Rider, Ronald Abbott

Stanley Baker (*Johnny Bannion*), Sam Wanamaker (*Mike Carter*), Margit Saad (*Suzanne*), Patrick Magee (*Chief Warder Barrows*), Grégoire Aslan (*Frank Saffron*), Jill Bennett (*Maggie*), Rupert Davies (*Mr. Edwards*), Laurence Naismith (*Mr. Town*), John Van Eyssen (*Formby*), Noel Willman (*Prison Governor*), Derek Francis (*Priest*), Redmond Phillips (*Prison Doctor*), Kenneth J. Warren (*Clobber*), Kenneth Cope (*Kelly*), Patrick Wymark (*Sol*), Jack Rodney (*Scout*), Murray Melvin (*Antlers*), John Molloy (*Snipe*), Brian Phelan (*Pauly Larkin*), Paul Stassino (*Alfredo Fanucci*), Jerold Wells (*Warder Brown*), Tom Bell (*Flynn*), Neil McCarthy (*O'Hara*), Keith Smith (*Hanson*), Nigel Green (*Ted*), Tom Gerard (*Quantock*), Larry Taylor (*Chas*), Sydney Bromley (*Frightened Prisoner*), Luigi Tiano (*Italian-speaking Prisoner*), Edward Judd (*Young Warder*), Richard Shaw (*Warder in Van*), Charles Lamb (*Mr. Able*), Maxwell Shaw (*1st Man at Party*), Victor Beaumont (*2nd Man at Party*), Dorothy Bromiley (*Angela*), Ronald Brittain (*Kitchen Warder*), Tommy Eytle (*West Indian Prisoner*), Dickie Owen (*1st Man in Prison*), Roy Dotrice (*Nicholls*), Bobby R. Naidoo (*Serang*), Maitland Williams (*West Indian Prisoner*).

Filmed at Merton Park Studios, Shepperton Studios and on location in London, December 1959–January 1960. First shown at the Edinburgh Festival, 28 August 1960; London, 27 October 1960; U.S.A., May 1962. Running time, 97 mins. (86 mins. in U.S.A.)
Distributors: Anglo Amalgamated (G.B.), Fanfare (U.S.)
U.S. title: *The Concrete Jungle*

The Damned (1962)

Production Company	Hammer/Swallow
Executive Producer	Michael Carreras
Producer	Anthony Hinds
Associate Producer	Anthony Nelson-Keys
Production Manager	Don Weeks
Director	Joseph Losey

Assistant Director	John Peverall
Script	Evan Jones. Based on the novel *The Children of Light* by H. L. Lawrence
Director of Photography	Arthur Grant (Hammerscope)
Camera Operator	Anthony Heller
Supervising Editor	James Needs
Editor	Reginald Mills
Design Consultant	Richard MacDonald
Production Designer	Bernard Robinson
Art Director	Don Mingaye
Music	James Bernard
Musical Director	John Hollingsworth
Song "Black Leather Rock"	James Bernard, Evan Jones
Costumes	Mollie Arbuthnot
Sound	Jock May
Sculptures	Elizabeth Frink

Macdonald Carey (*Simon Wells*), Shirley Ann Field (*Joan*), Viveca Lindfors (*Freya Neilson*), Alexander Knox (*Bernard*), Oliver Reed (*King*), Walter Gotell (*Major Holland*), James Villiers (*Captain Gregory*), Thomas Kempinski (*Ted*), Kenneth Cope (*Sid*), Brian Oulton (*Mr. Dingle*), Barbara Everest (*Miss Lamont*), Alan McClelland (*Mr. Stuart*), James Maxwell (*Mr. Talbot*), Rachel Clay (*Victoria*), Caroline Sheldon (*Elizabeth*), Rebecca Dignam (*Anne*), Siobhan Taylor (*Mary*), Nicholas Clay (*Richard*), Kit Williams (*Henry*), Christopher Witty (*William*), David Palmer (*George*), John Thompson (*Charles*), David Gregory, Anthony Valentine, Larry Martyn, Leon Garcia and Jeremy Phillips (*Teddy-boys*), Edward Harvey, Neil Wilson, Fiona Duncan, Tommy Trinder.

Filmed on location at Weymouth and Portland Bill, and at Bray Studios, May–June 1961. First shown in London, May 1963; U.S.A., July 1965. Running time, 87 mins. (77 mins. in U.S.A.)
Distributors: Columbia (G.B./U.S.)
U.S. title: *These Are The Damned*

Eve (1962)

Production Company	Paris Film (Paris)/Interopa Film (Rome)
Producers	Robert and Raymond Hakim
Production Manager	Danilo Marciani
Director	Joseph Losey
Assistant Director	Guidarino Guidi
Script	Hugo Butler, Evan Jones. Based on the novel by James Hadley Chase

Director of Photography	Gianni Di Venanzo (Venice Festival sequence shot by Henri Decaë)
Editors	Reginald Beck, Franca Silvi
Art Directors	Richard MacDonald, Luigi Scaccianoce
Music	Michel Legrand
Musical Director	Carlo Savina
Song "Adam and Eve"	Michel Legrand; sung by Tony Middleton
Songs "Willow Weep for Me" and "Loveless Love"	sung by Billie Holiday
Jeanne Moreau's costumes	Pierre Cardin
Sound	Boistelle, Federico Savina

Jeanne Moreau (*Eve Olivier*), Stanley Baker (*Tyvian Jones*), Virna Lisi [voice dubbed by Anna Proclemer] (*Francesca Ferrara*), Giorgio Albertazzi (*Branco Malloni*), James Villiers (*Arthur McCormick*), Riccardo Garrone (*Michele*), Lisa Gastoni (*The Redhead*), Checco Rissone (*Pieri*), Enzo Fiermonte (*Enzo*), Nona Medici (*Anna Maria*), Alex Revides (*The Greek*), John Pepper (*The Little Boy*), Roberto Paoletti, Van Eicken, Evi Rigano, Ignazio Dolce, Peggy Guggenheim, Gilda Dahlberg, Joseph Losey, Vittorio De Sica.

Filmed on location in Venice and Rome. First shown in Paris, 3 October 1962 (having been withdrawn from the Venice Festival, September 1962); G.B., 18 July 1963; U.S.A., June 1965. Running time, 100 mins. (France), 111 mins. (G.B.), 115 mins. (U.S.A.). [As originally edited, *Eve* ran 155 mins., and was cut by Losey himself to 135 mins.; the version shown to the French press had been cut to 116 mins., and it was subsequently further cut to 100 mins. for the public screening; the completest known version—with English dialogue and Finnish subtitles—runs 118 mins.] Distributors: Gala (G.B.), Times Film Corporation (U.S.) Italian title: *Eva*

The Servant (1963)

Production Company	Springbok/Elstree
Producers	Joseph Losey, Norman Priggen
Production Manager	Teresa Bolland
Director	Joseph Losey
Assistant Director	Roy Stevens
Script	Harold Pinter. Based on the novel by Robin Maugham
Director of Photography	Douglas Slocombe
Camera Operator	Chic Waterson

Editor	Reginald Mills
Production Designer	Richard MacDonald
Art Director	Ted Clements
Music/Musical Director	John Dankworth
Song "All Gone"	sung by Cleo Laine
Costumes	Beatrice Dawson
Sound Supervisor	John Cox
Sound Editor	Gerry Hambling
Sound Recordist	Buster Ambler

Dirk Bogarde (*Hugo Barrett*), James Fox (*Tony*), Wendy Craig (*Susan*), Sarah Miles (*Vera*), Catherine Lacey (*Lady Mounset*), Richard Vernon (*Lord Mounset*), Ann Firbank (*Society Woman in restaurant*), Doris Knox (*Older Woman in restaurant*), Patrick Magee (*Bishop*), Alun Owen (*Curate*), Jill Melford (*Young Woman in restaurant*), Harold Pinter (*Young Man in restaurant*), Derek Tansley (*Head Waiter*), Gerry Duggan (*Waiter*), Brian Phelan (*Irishman in Pub*), Hazel Terry (*Woman in Big Hat*), Philippa Hare (*Girl in Bedroom*), Dorothy Bromiley (*Girl Outside Phone Box*), Colette Martin, Joanne Wake and Harriet Devine (*Her friends*), Alison Seebohm (*Girl in Pub*), Chris Williams (*Coffee Bar Cashier*), Bruce Wells (*Painter*), John Dankworth (*Band leader*), Davy Graham (*Guitarist*).

Filmed on location in London and at Shepperton Studios, January–March 1963. First shown at the Venice Film Festival, 3 September 1963; G.B., 14 November 1963; U.S.A., March 1964 (previously at the New York Film Festival, 16 September 1963). Running time, 115 mins. Distributors: Warner-Pathé (G.B.), Landau (U.S.)

King and Country (1964)

Production Company	B.H.E. Productions
Executive Producer	Daniel M. Angel
Producers	Norman Priggen, Joseph Losey
Associate Producer/ Production Manager	Richard Goodwin
Director	Joseph Losey
Assistant Director	Scott Wodehouse
Script	Evan Jones. From the play *Hamp* by John Wilson, based on a story by James Lansdale Hodson
Director of Photography	Denys Coop
Camera Operator	Chic Waterson

Editor	Reginald Mills
Design Consultant	Richard Macdonald
Art Director	Peter Mullins
Music/Musical Director	Larry Adler
Costumes	Roy Ponting
Sound Supervisor	John Cox
Sound Editor	Gerry Hambling
Sound Recordist	Buster Ambler

Dirk Bogarde (*Captain Hargreaves*), Tom Courtenay (*Pte. Hamp*), Leo McKern (*Captain O'Sullivan*), Barry Foster (*Lt. Webb*), James Villiers (*Captain Midgley*), Peter Copley (*Colonel*), Barry Justice (*Lt. Prescott*), Vivian Matalon (*Padre*), Jeremy Spenser (*Pte. Sparrow*), James Hunter (*Pte. Sykes*), David Cook (*Pte. Wilson*), Larry Taylor (*Sergeant-Major*), Jonah Seymour (*Corporal Hamilton*), Keith Buckley (*Corporal of the Guard*), Richard Arthure (*Guard 'Charlie'*), Derek Partridge (*Captain at Court Martial*), Brian Tipping (*Lieutenant at Court Martial*), Raymond Brody, Terry Palmer and Dan Cornwall (*Soldiers in Hamp's Platoon*).

Filmed at Shepperton Studios, May–June 1964. First shown at the Venice Film Festival, 5 September 1964; G.B., 3 December 1964 (previously at London Film Festival, 8 November 1964; U.S.A., September 1965 (previously at New York Film Festival, 23 September 1964). Running time, 86 mins.
Distributors: Warner-Pathé (G.B.), Allied Artists (U.S.)

Modesty Blaise (1966)

Production Company	Modesty Blaise Ltd.
Producer	Joseph Janni
Associate Producers	Norman Priggen, Michael Birkett
Production Manager	Ed Harper
Director	Joseph Losey
Assistant to Director	Carlo Lastricati
Assistant Directors	Gavrik Losey, Claude Watson
Script	Evan Jones. Based on the comic strip created by Peter O'Donnell and Jim Holdaway
Director of Photography	Jack Hildyard
Colour Process	Technicolor
Location Photography (Amsterdam sequences)	David Boulton
Camera Operator	Gerry Fisher

Editor	Reginald Beck
Production Designer	Richard MacDonald
Art Director	Jack Shampan
Music/Musical Director	John Dankworth
Songs "Modesty Blaise"	
and "We Should Have"	Benny Green, Evan Jones
Song "Modesty Blaise"	sung by David and Jonathan
Costumes	Beatrice Dawson
Sound Editors	John Cox, John Aldred
Sound Recordist	Buster Ambler

Monica Vitti (*Modesty Blaise*), Terence Stamp (*Willie Garvin*), Dirk Bogarde (*Gabriel*), Harry Andrews (*Sir Gerald Tarrant*), Michael Craig (*Paul Hagan*), Scilla Gabel (*Melina*), Tina Marquand (*Nicole*), Clive Revill (*McWhirter* and *Sheikh Abu Tahir*), Rossella Falk (*Mrs. Fothergill*), Joe Melia (*Crevier*), Lex Schoorel (*Walter*), Silvan (*The Great Pacco*), Jon Bluming (*Hans*), Roberto Bisacco (*Enrico*), Saro Urzì (*Basilio*), Giuseppe Paganelli (*Friar*), Alexander Knox (*Minister*), Michael Chow (*Weng*), Marcello Turilli (*Strauss*), John Karlsen (*Oleg*), Robin Fox (*Man who presses the doorbell*).

Filmed on location in Amsterdam, Sicily, Naples, London and Farnborough, and at Shepperton Studios, July–October 1965. First shown in London, 5 May 1966; U.S.A., June 1966. Running time, 119 mins. Distributors: 20th Century-Fox (G.B./U.S.)

Accident (1967)

Production Company	Royal Avenue Chelsea
Producers	Joseph Losey, Norman Priggen
Production Supervisor	Geoffrey Haine
Director	Joseph Losey
Assistant Director	Richard Dalton
Script	Harold Pinter. Based on the novel by Nicholas Mosley
Director of Photography	Gerry Fisher
Colour Process	Eastman Colour
Camera Operator	Derek Browne
Editor	Reginald Beck
Art Director	Carmen Dillon
Music/Musical Director	John Dankworth
Costumes	Beatrice Dawson
Sound Editor	Alan Bell
Sound Recordists	Simon Kaye, Gerry Humphreys

Dirk Bogarde (*Stephen*), Stanley Baker (*Charley*), Jacqueline Sassard (*Anna*), Michael York (*William*), Vivien Merchant (*Rosalind*), Delphine Seyrig (*Francesca*), Alexander Knox (*The Provost*), Ann Firbank (*Laura*), Brian Phelan (*Police Sergeant*), Terence Rigby (*Plain-clothes policeman*), Harold Pinter (*Mr. Bell*), Freddie Jones (*Frantic Man at TV Studio*), Jane Hillary (*TV Receptionist*), Jill Johnson (*Secretary*), Nicholas Mosley (*A Don*), Maxwell Findlater and Carole Caplin (*The Children*).

Filmed on location at Cobham, Oxford, London and Syon House, and at Twickenham Studios, July–September 1966. First shown in London, 9 February 1967; U.S.A., April 1967. Running time, 105 mins. Distributors: London Independent Producers/Monarch (G.B.), Cinema V (U.S.)

Boom (1968)

Production Company	Universal
Producers	John Heyman, Norman Priggen
Production Manager	Ottavio Oppo
Director	Joseph Losey
Assistant Director	Carlo Lastricati
Script	Tennessee Williams. Based on his own story, *Man, Bring This Up Road*
Director of Photography	Douglas Slocombe (Panavision)
Colour Process	Eastman Colour
Camera Operator	Chic Waterson
Editor	Reginald Beck
Production Designer	Richard MacDonald
Music	John Barry
Song	John Dankworth; sung by Georgie Fame
Costumes	Tiziani
Sound	Leslie Hammond

Elizabeth Taylor (*Flora Goforth*), Richard Burton (*Chris Flanders*), Noël Coward (*Witch of Capri*), Joanna Shimkus (*Blackie*), Michael Dunn (*Rudy*), Romolo Valli (*Dr Lullo*), Veronica Wells (*Simonetta*), Fernando Piazza (*Giulio*), Howard Taylor (*Journalist*), Gens Bloch (*Photographer*), Franco Pesce (*Villager*), Claudie Ettori (*Manicurist*), Sergio Carozzi, Giovanni Paganelli.

Filmed on location in Sardinia and at the Dino de Laurentiis Studios in Rome; August–October 1967. Distributors: Rank (G.B.)

Boom

Secret Ceremony (1968)

Production Company.	Universal
Producers	John Heyman, Norman Priggen
Production Manager	Geoffrey Haine
Director	Joseph Losey
Assistant Director	Richard Dalton
Script	George Tabori. Based on a story by Marco Denevi
Director of Photography	Gerry Fisher (Widescreen)
Colour Process	Eastman Colour
Camera Operator	Jimmy Turrell
Editor	Reginald Beck

Production Designer	Richard MacDonald
Art Director	John Clark
Set Decorator	Jill Oxley
Music	Richard Rodney Bennett
Costumes	Dior (for Elizabeth Taylor), Susan Yelland
Sound	Leslie Hammond

Elizabeth Taylor (*Leonora*), Mia Farrow (*Cenci*), Robert Mitchum (*Albert*), Pamela Brown (*Aunt Hilda*), Peggy Ashcroft (*Aunt Hanna*).

Filmed on location in London and at Associated British Studios, Elstree; shooting started 18 March 1968.
Distributors: Rank (G.B.)

Short Films

Pete Roleum and his Cousins (1939)

Production Company	Petroleum Industries Exhibition Inc. (New York)
Producer ⎫ Director ⎬ Script ⎭	Joseph Losey
Director of Photography	Harold Muller (3D)
Colour Process	Technicolor
Animation	Charles Bowers
Designer of Puppets	Howard Bay
Editor	Helen Van Dongen
Music	Hanns Eisler, Oscar Levant
Narrator	Hiram Sherman

The history and development of oil: a puppet film made for the New York World's Fair. Running time, 20 mins.

A Child Went Forth (1941)

Production Company	National Association of Nursery Educators (New York)
Producer/Director	Joseph Losey, John Ferno
Script	Joseph Losey
Director of Photography	John Ferno
Music	Hanns Eisler
Narrator	Munro Leaf

An exposition of the principles of progressive education, through the activities of children (aged 2–7) at the Nell Goldsmith nursery camp, Woodlea. Running time, 18 mins.

Youth Gets a Break (1941)

Production Company	National Youth Administration
Director	Joseph Losey (directing one of three crews)
Script	Joseph Losey
Directors of Photography	John Ferno, Willard Van Dyke, Ralph Stevens

Running time, 20 mins.

A Gun in his Hand (1945)

Production Company	M-G-M
Director	Joseph Losey
Script	Charles Francis Royal. Based on a story by Richard Landau
Director of Photography	Jackson Rose
Editor	Harry Komer
Art Director	Richard Duce
Music	Max Terr

Anthony Caruso (*Pinky*), Richard Gaines (*Inspector Dana*), Ray Teal (*O'Neill*).

A film in the "Crime Does Not Pay" series. Running time, 19 mins.

A Man on the Beach (1955)

Production Company	Hammer Films
Producer	Anthony Hinds
Production Manager	Michael Delamar
Director	Joseph Losey
Assistant Director	Denis Bertera
Script	Jimmy Sangster. Based on a story *Chance at the Wheel* by Victor Canning
Director of Photography	Wilkie Cooper (Cinepanorama)
Colour Process	Eastman Colour
Camera Operator/location photography	Len Harris
Editor	Henry Richardson

Design Consultant	Richard MacDonald
Art Director	Edward Marshall
Music	John Hotchkis
Sound	W. H. P. May

Donald Wolfit (*Carter*), Michael Medwin (*Max*), Michael Ripper (*Chauffeur*), Alex de Gallier (*Casino Manager*), Edward Forsyth (*Clement*), Krik S. Siegenburg (*Little Boy*), Shandra Walden (*Little Girl*), Barry Shawzin (*The American*), Nora Maiden and Corinne Grey (*Girls on the Beach*).

Running time, 29 mins.

First on the Road (1960)

Production Company	Graphic Films for Ford Motors
Producer	Leon Clore
Director	Joseph Losey
Director of Photography	Larry Pizer
Colour Process	Technicolor
Music	Frank Cordell

A sponsored short illustrating, with jazz accompaniment but no commentary, the features of the 1960 Anglia Saloon. Running time, 12 mins.

Stage Productions

1933 *Little Ol' Boy* by Albert Bein (Playhouse, New York, 24 April)

1934 *Jayhawker* by Sinclair Lewis and Lloyd Lewis (Cort Theatre, New York, 5 November; previously at Washington and Philadelphia)
A Bride for the Unicorn by Denis Johnston (Brattleboro Theatre, Cambridge, Mass.)
Gods of the Lightning by Maxwell Anderson (Peabody Theatre, Boston)

1935 *Waiting for Lefty* by Clifford Odets (in Moscow, with English-speaking actors)

1936 *Hymn to the Rising Sun* by Paul Green (Theatre Union at Civic Repertory Theatre, 12 January)
The Living Newspaper (Various programmes: Federal Theatre at Biltmore Theatre, New York)
Who Fights This Battle? by Kenneth White (Federal Theatre, staged in New York hotel ballroom)
Conjur Man Dies by Rudolph Fischer (Federal Theatre at Lafayette Theatre, New York, 11 March)

1937 Director of the "Political Cabaret"

1938 *Sunup to Sundown* by Frances Faragoh (Hudson Theatre, New York, 1 February)

1940–43 Staged various War Relief Shows in New York, Washington, Boston, Philadelphia, Chicago, Detroit; director of "The Lunch Hour Follies"

1945 Staged Roosevelt Memorial Show at the Hollywood Bowl

1946 Staged Academy Award Show at Grauman's Chinese Theatre, Hollywood

1947 *The Great Campaign* by Arnold Sundgaard (Princess Theatre, New York, 30 March)
Galileo by Bertold Brecht (Coronet Theatre, Los Angeles, August)
Galileo by Bertold Brecht (Maxine Elliott Theatre, New York, 7 December)

1954 *The Wooden Dish* by Edmund Morris (Phoenix Theatre, London, 27 July)

1955 *The Night of the Ball* by Michael Burn (New Theatre, London, 12 January)

Acknowledgements

Grateful thanks for stills are due to:

Anglo Amalgamated (*The Sleeping Tiger*, *The Intimate Stranger*, *The Criminal*); Columbia (*The Damned*, *M*, *The Big Night*); Eros Films (*Time Without Pity*); Gala Film Distributors (*Eve*); Monarch Film Corporation (*Accident*); Paramount (*The Dividing Line*); Rank Film Distributors (*The Gypsy and the Gentleman*); Rank and David Deutsch (*Blind Date*); RKO-Radio (*The Boy with Green Hair*); 20th Century-Fox (*Modesty Blaise*); United Artists (*The Big Night*); United Artists and Horizon Pictures (*The Prowler*); Warner-Pathé (*The Servant*, *King and Country*); Radio Times Hulton Picture Library (*The Wooden Dish*).
To Joseph Losey, John Hubley and Richard MacDonald for *The Prowler* and *The Sleeping Tiger* sketches.
To Cedric Pheasant for frame stills from *Eve*.
To the National Film Archive and the Cinémathèque Royale de Belgique for their help in obtaining stills.